ABRAHAM'S SON

The Making of an American

HENRY D. SCHUSTER
WITH CAROLINE A. ORZES

PublishAmerica
Baltimore

First printing

PublishAmerica has allowed this work to remain exactly as the author intended, verbatim, without editorial input.

Hardcover 978-1-4560-0521-4
Softcover 978-1-4489-5760-6
PUBLISHED BY PUBLISHAMERICA, LLLP
www.publishamerica.com
Baltimore

Printed in the United States of America

DEDICATION

I dedicate this book to the 33 people from the town of my birth, Sterbfritz, Germany, who were murdered by the Nazis, including my mother, Rosa Schuster, and my sister, Margot Schuster.

Also to my wife, Anita, for her love and devotion for more than 60 years, and for the endless hours she spent sitting at the computer editing my memoir.

To my sister, Bertel, who survived the brutality of the Holocaust for four years, and who has become my best friend.

To our children, grandchildren and great-grandchildren, who are my world.

FOREWORD

As a small boy growing up in an almost idyllic life in a small German town in the pre-World War II days of the late 1920s and early 1930s, I never could have foreseen what happened to me—that I would not live my life in Germany but in America; that English, not German, would be the language I would speak daily; and that I would live out my later years in Las Vegas, Nevada, an American Southwest city that at the time was nothing more than a bend in the road. More immediately, I could never have forecast the ugly hatred that was to envelop my country and my town. Nor could I have foreseen the evil that invaded the minds and souls of many, if not all my non-Jewish friends who during the Hitler years came to hate me and other Jews vehemently. Why those who did not share the hatred said nothing, did nothing, is even more inconceivable. But I have to accept that it happened because I was there. I witnessed it. I saw it firsthand, and I like so many others, lost family and friends in the Holocaust that transpired.

I was one of the lucky ones. Too young to save myself, I was saved by others. Strangers who risked their lives to safeguard mine and hundreds of other Jewish children's lives when Hitler rounded up thousands of men, women and children to be exterminated or worked to death in camps all over Europe. In the chaos that ensued, I was literally swooped up by caring people who took me out of harm's way and out of Germany to France, a temporary asylum, and later to a permanent refuge in the United States.

I was not a brave child; fear gripped me almost constantly, and I cried deeply into my pillow at night, embarrassed by my weakness and hoping no one would hear. My father already dead, I had never been separated from my family before. I have vivid memories of gut-wrenching terror not only for myself, but for my mother and sisters who were left behind. It was years before I learned what happened to them; years before I could stop the nightmares; years before I could stop feeling survivor guilt, the guilt from having lived when people I so dearly loved endured brutality and death. I often wish I had never learned how they died, for I can picture it so vividly in my mind. The horror lingers to this day.

Many books have been brilliantly written about the Holocaust, but this book is about more than the horrors. Mine is a success story—a story about successfully evading and outliving Nazi murderers and creating a wonderful life. It's about a life that flies in the face of Hitler's plan to exterminate all Jews. It's about overcoming obstacles to create a new and purposeful life in America as a contributing American citizen. It's about a boy who became a man, and a man who became an American soldier, a husband and father, businessman and later an organizer of other Holocaust survivors.

In short, it's about the making of an American. But it's also about human kindness. It's about the sort of kindness that rises to the surface even in, maybe especially in, times of appalling evil. It's about my odyssey to sanctuary in the United States, and about the many brave people who risked their own and their family's lives to save my life and the lives of so many hundreds of other children—children they didn't even know.

Most important, it's about thankfulness. There are so many people to thank. People like the hundreds of selfless Quakers whose religion would not allow them to tolerate the murder of millions of people, the people of *Oeuvre de Secours Aux Enfants* (OSE) and the Joint Distribution Committee—people whose names I never knew and never will know. But the names I know and remember, and I hope the world remembers, are: Isador Marks (whom I called uncle, though he was no relation to me) and who was the director of the Rothschild orphanage in Frankfurt along with his wife, Rosa, whom I also affectionately called aunt; Ernst Papanek and Dr. Helena Papanek—teachers, healers, rescuers and respected benefactors; Boris Genoitman, a Russian Jew who was counsellor and director of the French Orthodox children's home where I was housed after fleeing Germany; the Baroness de Rothschild, who placed Jewish children in orphanages for their own safety and who lovingly kept our minds off the horror of the war with entertaining excursions and entertainment; Eleanor Roosevelt, who after the shameful S.S. St. Louis disaster, where 900 Jewish refugees were denied entrance into the United States only to be returned to Europe where they were murdered by Hitler's henchmen, later prevailed upon her husband President Franklin Delano Roosevelt to allow rescued Jewish children to enter the United States; and Marshall Field, famous for heading up a successful department store empire but lesser known for his valiant efforts to put his fortune to good use saving hundreds of Jewish lives. To each one I owe a debt I could never repay. Nor would they wish to be repaid, for brave people see their deeds as nothing out of the ordinary, universally and erroneously believing that "anyone would have done it."

My gratitude for these brave souls was never stronger then when I watched my own children being born and then growing into self-sufficient adults. They would never have had life if mine had been extinguished so many years ago in Germany, so they, too, are indebted. So many in the debt of so few. In Judaism, we believe that to save one life is to save the world, a concept that has taken me 70-odd years to fully understand. My beautiful family is my world—children, grandchildren, and now even great-grandchildren who would never be living, breathing human beings had I not been saved. That thought alone rid me of the survivor guilt I possessed for so many years.

I survived for a reason: to become an American citizen and serve my adopted country well through military service and a career of hard work and contribution. My wife, Anita, and I gave life to children who in turn gave life to their children. In the years to come, hundreds of Jewish men and woman will carry on the traditions and faith of our ancestors because I survived. It's an awesome thought, but one that makes my ordeal bearable, and my heart thankful. This book is my story.

Henry D. Schuster
Las Vegas, Nevada
January 2010

CHAPTER
ONE

In June 1918, the German government signed the Treaty of Versailles, which officially ended World War I. Though the battlefields were now quiet, Europe's cities were broken and her financial and commercial institutions were shattered. Attempting to restore economic order, in April 1922, thirty-four nations assembled in Genoa, Italy. The task was destined to fail because at the same time, in Rapallo, Italy, German and Soviet Union representatives were formulating a private agreement, one that would permit the rebuilding of the German military by secretly allowing Germany to manufacture armaments, armaments that were strictly forbidden by the Treaty of Versailles, inside Soviet borders. When the Treaty of Rapallo was announced, it undermined the Genoa negotiations. Seeing that further endeavors were pointless, the conference disbanded on May 19, 1922.

Sterbfritz, Germany

It was October 18, 1922 and Abraham Schuster was angry. He was so angry he wouldn't talk to his wife, Rosa, who had just given birth to a girl. Not just *a* girl, *another* girl. He wondered if Rosa would *ever* give him a boy. More than anything, he longed for a son he could name after his father as was Jewish custom. Maybe next time it would happen. Rosa was young and could bear more children. "It will happen next time," he sighed in resignation.

And it did. On March 18, 1926, the house at 24 Schlüchterner Strasse, Sterbfritz, Kreis Schlüchtern, Germany rejoiced with my birth. I, Heinz Dittmar Schuster, was born. Red faced from the indignity of the birthing process, I came into this world—the longed-for male child who would be cuddled and coddled by my mother, kissed and petted by my sisters, Bertel and Margot, and proudly proffered for admiration to family, friends and strangers by my father. As the third and last child, and Rosa and Abraham's only male offspring, I knew from the start I held an enviable position in the family hierarchy. As they say, life was good.

From the beginning, I was aware I was Mother's favorite. In her eyes, I could do no wrong, a circumstance I relished and often took advantage of. My father wasn't nearly as besotted with my cuteness, nor was he as easily manipulated by my innocent face and winning ways. Pouting and whining got me nowhere with Father who, you see, had been a boy himself; and he had brothers. He knew the game; he was impossible to get around.

But in his own quiet and reserved way, he, too, doted on me and loved me. He relished showing me off to friends, shopkeepers and people on the street he hardly knew. When I got older, he proudly walked with me, hand-in-hand. I toddled along with him to the barbershop for his Friday-before-the-Sabbath shave, where once in a while the luxury of a haircut was added to the weekly ritual. It was easy to keep up because a bout with typhus in his younger years left Father's feet damaged and made walking painful. But, off we went, probably a comical sight, father and son doddering similarly down the street.

I revered my father, whose sheer size put me on my best behavior and made strangers take respectful notice. Long limbed and heavyset, the tallest of his six siblings and bigger than most men, he cut an impressive figure. I was in awe of him. His massive size, however, belied his congenial nature. Shy and soft-spoken, he was a gentle man and a loving husband and father. In the community, he made friends easily and maintained those friendships, both Jewish and Christian, throughout his entire life. Everyone liked my father and in today's jargon, he would have been happy to be referred to as "one of the boys."

He was the best father. My sisters and I loved him because he was just a big kid himself and was always looking for things to do to entertain us. One cold, snowy December day, he took his beloved horse, Frieda, and hitched her to a sleigh. The joy of his life, Frieda had been groomed for hours until her coat gleamed, and black had been applied to darken and shine her hooves. She was a beautiful sight as she drew near the house pulling the shiny sleight. One-by-one, Father loaded us onto the leather seats in back, carefully laying woolen blankets over our laps and legs. I remember looking up and seeing tree branches glisten icily and the snow in the fields sparkling in the sun like a blanket of diamonds.

Racing through the snow-packed streets, trees, houses, cows and sheep whipping by, we giggled and squealed with joy, the crisp, cold air coloring our faces pink and shiny. Roused by our laughter, Father cracked his whip to make Frieda go faster and faster. Then an ice patch hidden under the snow caught the sleigh blades, and the sleigh skidded sideways for yards until it toppled into a ditch. Luckily, both horse and passengers were unharmed, and we tumbled out of the sleigh, knee-deep in the snow. Guiding the horse by the reins, Father slowly led her back onto the road, sleigh trailing behind. Everything and everybody was okay. No damage was done, and it was a rollicking good time!

Sterbfritz was, and still is, a small town nestled in the Taunus Mountain Range in the province of Hesse. It was probably typical of small German mountain towns of the era, but being young and with no way to compare I can only guess that Sterbfritz was not unique. It was a quaint life compared with today. Even as late as the mid-1920s and despite the availability of newsprint, as in medieval times Sterbfritz employed a town crier. Mr. Heil, Sterbfritz' crier, would amble to the center of town once a day—or more often if it was a big-news day. The ringing of his hand-held bell announced a newsworthy event was about to be revealed. The bell was the envy of all, a finely constructed artifact made of brass with a tooled and polished wooden handle. Old Mr. Heil rang the bell repeatedly in order to allow Sterbfritz citizens time to gather 'round. Then, in the most solemn voice, he read the particulars of the latest news flash. It could be anything from the arrival of a baby to the arrival of a calf or piglet. Undoubtedly, my arrival years before warranted this kind of announcement.

Despite an anachronism like a town crier and despite the smallness of its size, Sterbfritz was not backward. Sterbfritz had not one, but two schools—a public school and a Jewish parochial one-room schoolhouse. It also had a church as well as a synagogue. The town hall, an efficient-looking, sturdy two-story brick building, stood on Brückenauer Strasse, and was the place where the mayor, who was elected for a 10-year term, presided. The town's lone policeman was an employee of the state, not the town as would be expected, and the jail, which was located over the public bull stable, was used mostly to detain citizens while they sobered up. Real crimes didn't happen in Sterbfritz.

The town was then home to about 1,300 souls,—1,190 Protestant, 100 Jewish, and 10 Catholic, give or take. Religious differences meant little then, at least in my scope of things. It seemed that good character and an enterprising nature were the yardsticks by which men, and women, were judged. We, the Schusters, were judged well.

As well we should. Most Sterbfritz families were poor, barely eking out a daily living, literally a hand-to-mouth existence. My parents were industrious and because of their enterprise fared better than most. Through sheer hard work, they were able to earn a comfortable living, and in 1919, shortly after WWI, my father built the house we were to live in, a luxury dwelling—three stories tall and one of only five houses in the entire town that had indoor flushing toilets. Our house had not only had one, but incredibly, *two* flushing toilets.

The two upper floors were the living quarters, but the ground floor was planned to be a store, specifically a grocery store would sell much more than food. Shoes, clothing and household items would be found on the shelves. It was a business my mother ran and it not only provided the best kosher food in town, on cold winter mornings it was a place where neighbors gathered to catch up on local gossip—much of which came to Sterbfritz via my father's business travels.

Father's primary job was furniture sales, but his unofficial job was to carry the news back and forth between the town and countryside. Summer, winter, spring and fall, Abram (as he was called for short) Schuster was the purveyor of fine furniture, fine fabrics, goodwill, and most important, news.

Father was a traveling furniture, farm implement and yard goods vendor who journeyed by horse and carriage, sometimes train, to farms and outlying towns to sell his merchandise. His furniture orders were filled by the local *tischler knauf* (furniture maker), who custom built the furniture items that he sold. If the exact design was not to be found in the catalogues, the manufacturer would, for a slightly higher fee, alter the design to suit the buyer's wishes. My father was an expert at listening to customers' needs, then drawing the design on paper that would be followed to a "T" by the manufacturer.

In addition to furniture catalogues, Father carried fabric swatches that ladies could inspect and choose from for dresses, window coverings, slip covers and the like. Once a fabric was chosen, my father returned home, cut the desired length from bolts he kept in the storeroom, then delivered them on his return trip.

Father must have been a welcome sight, peculiar as he might have seemed loaded down with manufacturer's catalogues. His were more than just catalogs, however. They were dream books whose pages were filled with black and white drawings of beds, night tables and vanities; dining tables, sideboards and highboys; settees, ottomans and chairs. He had something for every room in the house as well as every pocketbook. His catalogues were filled with the stuff both seasoned housewives and newlywed brides dreamed of and were sometimes able to buy.

But while the business put bread on the table, Father was a farmer at heart and longed to work his land. Squatting by the edge of his fields that overlooked the town, I often saw him sift the dark, loamy soil through his fingers, soil that produced the best oats, rye and wheat in Germany, grains that were to become stone-ground flour at the gristmill then kneaded and twisted into loaves of all varieties and shapes. German breads made by German hands that were the best in the world.

He wasn't able to pursue his dream of working the land because it didn't pay enough, and Father was an ambitious man. Instead, he was a gentleman farmer, hiring "a man" to do the backbreaking labor of plowing the fields and tending the livestock.

Father also kept sheep, which were set to graze in a large field outside of town and were overseen by a shepherd my father paid. The shepherd tended the sheep by day and by night he slept with his dogs in a wagon stationed in the middle of the field.

Each spring, the shepherd drove the flock to town—to the yard that surrounded our house—for shearing and lambing. Hired women sheared the sheep of the heavy wool they had grown in the cold winter months. Lambs were born and later they would make the long march back to the grazing field where they would remain until the following spring. All the farmers herded their sheep to the shearers where the new-born lambs were branded, a process not unlike cattle branding in the American West though the branding took place on their ears instead of their flanks. I only heard about the branding because children weren't allowed to witness it.

As hard as my father worked, my recollection is that my mother worked even harder. Along with the regular maintenance of the house, her main responsibility was running the store, seeing the inventory was kept up, stock ordered and produce arranged appealingly. The workday was long, but a bell over the shop door gave Mother the freedom to tend to household chores when not taking care of customers. The bell's ringing meant there was a customer, and with a sweep of her long skirts she breezed into the store through the kitchen door and took care of business.

Once, Mother noticed certain items missing from the candy bin. Never able to pinpoint who was in the store when the items went missing, Mother gave up trying to find the culprit. My sister Bertel, on the other hand, wouldn't rest until she found out who had sticky fingers and devised a plan to catch the thief.

Hiding under a cloth-covered table in the corner of the store for what must have been hours, she patiently waited. An eternity later, a neighbor girl slowly opened the store's door and as she did so she held the bell so it wouldn't ring. The girl crept through the door, then tiptoed silently behind the counter to the candy bin. Reaching into the bin, she was just about to fill her apron with candy when Bertel jumped from under the table and grabbed her arm, catching the thief red-handed with fists full of candy. Squealing and squirming to get free, she spilled the candy all over the floor and fled through the shop door, this time the bell rang wildly. That was the end of the missing items. Bertel had saved the day.

But more than the day-to-day routine of running a busy shop, Mother shared some of the backbreaking farm labor with the hired man. In planting season, she temporarily entrusted the store's safekeeping to my two sisters, then trudged the well-worn path to the fields, a gunnysack filled with seed potatoes slung over her shoulder. Following the horse-drawn plow, she carefully lifted each potato wedge from the sack and placed it in the furrow. I still remember her bent-over form, placing potato pieces just right so they would grow up, not down, the setting sun illuminating her bonnet like a halo. I loved planting time. I loved to watch the plowing, the sweat-browned flanks of the plow horse, the warmth of the sun and the musky smell of freshly turned earth as the plow carved a crease in the soil. It was heaven.

Maybe it was because I was little and still at home with my mother that I saw how much work she did. Every Sunday was washday where clothes were nearly washboarded to shreds in the attempt to get them as clean and bright as new. Mother took pride in having the cleanest, whitest laundry in town. After washing, the wet clothes were hung on the line to dry—summer and winter. In summer, they flapped in the breeze and the fresh air smell permeated the fabric like ozone perfume. In winter, the clothes often froze before they dried, a condition I found hilarious. Nothing was funnier to my 5-year-old sense of humor than frozen long johns. Unless, of course, it was my sisters' frozen pantaloons. No worry. Mother assured us they would eventually "freeze dry," a phenomenon that would have made us rich had we been knowledgeable enough to apply it to coffee.

I knew summer was nearing its end when Mother hauled the canning tubs and jars from the basement to the kitchen. Then the work of washing fruit and vegetables, cutting, coring and blanching the plums, peaches, apples, tomatoes, beans and cucumbers in preparation for canning began. I remember with awe my mother expertly ladling the cooked fruit and vegetables into steaming hot jars that were quickly capped with shiny metal lids and just as quickly turned upside down to form a tight seal while cooling. Rows of colorful jars eventually lined the kitchen, later to be taken to the cold cellar beneath the house and neatly stacked on wooden shelves. The cold cellar was a place I loved to hide in not only because it was a chilly reprieve from the hot summer sun, but because its darkness and earthy smell conjured up awesome fantasies and make believe for an imaginative 5 year old. It was heaven.

Schusters had been in Sterbfritz a long time, since 1643 to be exact, a fact verified with easy research into well-kept town records. I was boyishly proud that a Schuster was one of the first to be buried in the Jewish cemetery in the neighboring town of Altengronau, and though little is known about the Schuster buried there, chances are he was one of the *Schutz Juden* (protected Jews) brought to the town by Christian noblemen to be moneylenders or bookkeepers.

Whoever he was, we were glad he was one of ours. His grave, the headstone weathered and pitted by the elements even then, lent us a history, a sort of legitimacy, a claim to the land. It was comforting to know a Schuster had been there long before I was born. It was comforting to think there would be Schusters in Sterbfritz long after my immediate family was gone.

Little Sterbfritz was always a hubbub of activity, but Sunday afternoons were especially lively. Of the three bakeries in town, the Jewish-owned bakery and café, was the most rowdy, and consequently the place we liked the best. Not only could adults, both Christian and Jewish, join in a spirited game of cards, we kids could always con a parent or two into buying us ice cream. That, or a fabulously fragrant, fresh-baked cinnamon roll that put olfactory nerves into frenzy and taste buds into delirium—ecstasy to the nose and tongue.

Not at all a backward town, Sterbfritz boasted the latest in amenities. Health care was available to all, for a fair fee, with two doctors and a Catholic dentist, Dr. Reinhardt. I went to school with Dr. Reinhardt's children and knew them well. Later Dr. Reinhardt would place his own life and the lives of his family in jeopardy by refusing to comply with Nazi laws that forbid gentile health care practitioners from treating Jews. If a Jewish patient had a toothache, Dr. Reinhardt would smuggle them into his basement after dark. It was there he installed another dental chair, one that would be used for his Jewish patients only. Dr. Reinhardt refused to bow down to the Nazi mandates and continued to treat Jewish patients and relieve them from dental pain.

Sterbfritz also had a nurse practitioner, and I remember seeing her shingle outside a small room over the town post office, a place that not only handled mail delivery but also was the stop for the lone bus that came through town twice a week. The post office was the town's communications hub because in addition to mail delivery and the bus stop it housed the town's only telephone, a device that was used by everyone. The joke was that if you talked loudly enough into the phone, as almost everybody did, you wouldn't need the phone at all.

Sterbfritz was proud to have two gas stations as well as two auto repair shops, establishments that had no trouble serving the needs of the entire town because hardly anyone owned a car. But almost everyone who didn't own a car owned a horse, or even two horses, so the town smithy did a brisk business. Horses are notorious for repeat business in the shoeing department. If they weren't throwing shoes they needed periodic shoe replacement because the hoof grew out so much it needed to be pared. That required removing the old shoe and replacing it with a newer, shinier shoe. It was a never-ending process that earned a good living for the smithy.

Vivid memories of our home flood over me even now, so many years removed. Memories triggered instantly by smells and aromas of good things to eat that remind me of dishes Mother prepared in our kitchen, a warm, inviting place where the family gathered in winter for warmth, conversation and laughter. In summer, it was the place to enjoy the rush of cooling breezes when doors and windows were opened to the world. In summer, it seemed as if the kitchen windows never closed, the crisp white curtains ruffling in the air.

Often, sparrows perched on the sills eying the room for an easy breakfast or lunch, but no bird ever risked life or wing to enter. That is, until a huge black crow established his position on the sill. The glint of a silver spoon in the sunlight caught this brazen fellow's attention. Eying the shiny treasure from his perch on the sill, he couldn't resist seizing the first opportunity to capture his prize. With one circuitous swoop through the kitchen, he grabbed his treasure and soared back through the open window and was gone, the silver spoon in his beak glinting as he made his way to his nest high atop the trees. We never found the spoon, so it must still reside somewhere in the tree branches. It was a story my father loved to tell and retell over the years, and one that still makes me smile to remember.

The "breakfast table," so named because we always ate breakfast there, was the only table in the kitchen, and the place where we actually ate all our meals—breakfast, lunch and dinner. It was the place where the eight surrounding chairs were often occupied by family and friends as they broke bread and shared the news of the day. Warmed by a wood-burning stove in the winter, the kitchen was made even more inviting by a long, wooden storage bench that comfortably sat two adults or three wriggling children. When people weren't sitting on it, it doubled as a sort of toy box, a place where abandoned toys were stashed.

Pots and pans galore filled the cupboards; many were made from cast iron, seasoned black by fragrant meals that simmered for hours. Aluminum pots were a second-best choice, but also used so frequently and for so many years that they, at times, sprung leaks, an event that called for a trip to the smithy. Once the offending hole was soldered, it was almost as good as new, and it was placed back into service with the rest of the cookware.

The pantry, always bursting with jars, boxes and bins filled with provisions was a testament to our prosperity and industry. Everyone had a job to do, and mine was to fetch ingredients for dinner from the basement where even more shelves, bins and crocks were to be found. Apples, pears and potatoes were stored there for the winter, and it would not be unusual to find pickled briskets in earthenware crocks covered by wooden lids. We had more food than we could eat, and much of it remained in the pantry more than a year. But, nothing went to waste, a sin in itself, and Mother employed a rotation system to make sure the oldest jars were used first.

Everyone in the Jewish community was Orthodox, which meant we kept strictly kosher and we, like many other Jewish families, butchered our own animals to ensure they were slaughtered according to scripture. A ritual slaughterer, called a *shochet*, made the rounds performing the ancient ritual, a sight I was not allowed to witness until I was older. But I remember one cold winter day when I was old enough, my father bought a quarter beef from the kosher butcher who arriving with block and grinder in hand and began the process of grinding the beef.

The large grinding machine with its pulley and the wheels fascinated me. It was the best thing I had ever seen in my life so far—watching the meat slabs crammed into the grinder with a wooden pusher, only to come out the other end in fat, pink strings. Next, my mother scooped it up with her hands and put it in a huge crockery bowl, salting and spicing it to make the sausage. All the kids loved the butcher not only because we wanted to *be* butchers when we grew up, but mostly because he gave us pieces of hard candy from a little tin box in his pocket. It was heaven.

Though animals may be slaughtered according to Jewish law, the meat is not considered kosher until all traces of blood are removed, it's salted and then let to stand for several hours. Once, my mother followed the custom and placed the meat in a special wicker basket at our kitchen window. It was Friday, and as she did her usual pre-Sabbath cleaning, she stood on a kitchen chair to dust the upper part of one of the kitchen windows. Leaning too far over, the chair tipped and she tumbled off onto the floor, en route knocking the meat and bones from the basket all over herself. Hearing the crash, I raced to the kitchen only to see Mother sitting on the floor surrounded by the carnage. I rushed to help her, crying hystericaly because I thought what I saw was my mother's leg, bloody and in pieces on the floor. Still sitting in the spillage, she laughed and gathered me up, holding me, kissing my hair and assuring me everything was all right. Mother's kisses always made the world right again.

Like many places in the world, people in Sterbfritz did what they could to make a living. One such enterprising person was the tailor Mack. Now, the tailoring business must not have been very lucrative or Mack may not have been a very good tailor, because Mack seemed only able to make a meager living from his tailoring business. To supplement his income, Mack decided to become the town's pig herder, and every morning he walked the streets blowing his horn, pigs following him in the style of snakes following St.

Patrick in Ireland. The townspeople, thinking that someone else taking care of their pigs was a jolly good idea, opened their pigpens and let the animals out to follow Mack, better known as the *Sauhirt* (pig herder), into the neighboring fields to wallow in the mud all day and munch on whatever they could find to eat. Come late afternoon, Mack collected the pigs and herded them up the street to their pens. Fortunately for Mack, who couldn't tell one pig from the other, the pigs were smart enough to know where they lived, and each veered off to his own pen at the right time. Ne'er was a pig lost or sent to the wrong household.

For the Sterbfritz kids this was joke fodder, and Mack became the brunt of our childish humor. Having had enough of the ridicule, the Sauhirt evened the playing field by brandishing a small pocketknife, or maybe his tailoring scissors, I don't remember which, and threatened to remove our ears with it. Making believe he was slicing off ears, he'd run after us until we scattered and hid. Once, when I was particularly slow, Mack caught me and pinched my ears so hard I thought he'd actually cut them off. I ran home screaming in pain and ran to the open arms of my sister Bertel who checked both sides of my head and declared that, miraculously, I still had both ears. Once I assured myself she was right, the pain stopped, and I was able to hear again. A miracle had happened.

CHAPTER
TWO

Mother's maiden name was Steinfeld, Theresa Steinfeld, but for reasons unknown to me she was called Rosa. In 1892, she was born in the hamlet of Josbach, the fifth child of Herz and Johanna Steinfeld—a family that would ultimately have four boys and three girls. If there is such a thing as a favorite child, it certainly was Rosa. All her siblings admired her and my grandparents doted on her. Upon completion of her eighth year of education, she was sent to a finishing school, common for girls at the time, in the city of Marburg where she got a solid education in the three "Rs." Her talent for storytelling, in addition to her ability to write and recite poetry, was noteworthy and highly encouraged at the school. Mother would have made a wonderful public speaker for she had a gift for telling riveting stories and had a new one for every occasion. Her story telling was often the main entertainment at social gatherings.

Soon after graduation, Rosa returned to Josbach, and with no marriage proposals that she would seriously consider at hand, she helped her father with his business endeavors. But it wouldn't be long before Mother had a proposal that was worth her consideration.

Not far from Josbach lived the Blumenfeld family—distant relatives of the Steinfelds. Handsome young Moritz Blumenfeld was just two years older than Rosa, and after Sabbath services the three Blumenfeld children and several Steinfelds walked halfway the distance between to meet. Moritz and Rosa were immediately attracted to each other, quickly became a pair, and soon the couple began to talk of marriage.

But fate stepped in before plans could materialize. World War I was raging and Moritz was inducted into the German army. Not long after, Rosa got word he had been captured by the British. No one knew where he was or even if he was alive. She was devastated. Even if he were still alive, there was no way to know when he would be released, if ever, and time was marching on. Heartbroken though she was, Rosa was a pragmatic young woman. She was 26 years old, and in today's vernacular her biological clock was ticking. All her girlfriends were married or spoken for. Some even had babies. Time was *not* on her side, and besides, there were other fish in the sea. Rosa set out to find another fellow.

Toni Blumenfeld, the oldest of the Blumenfeld brood, was now married to Moritz Schuster who also lived in Sterbfritz. As luck would have it, bachelor Abraham Schuster, Toni's brother-in-law, was looking for a wife, and Toni made a recommendation to the Steinfelds. "Maybe Rosa should meet Abraham," they said. Since the captured Moritz Blumenfeld's future was uncertain, pragmatic Rosa had no objection to meeting young Mr. Schuster.

At that time, many German-Jewish marriages were arranged by either professional matchmakers or through friends and family, and Herz Steinfeld began the footwork required to see if a match was in order. Would this Abraham Schuster fellow be worthy of his daughter? He didn't want to be too blunt and make a direct inquiry, so Herz Steinfeld traveled to Sterbfritz to visit his relative, Toni. With the excuse that he was in the area for business, Toni introduced Herz to the prospective suitor. Abraham must have passed muster because both felt that a Rosa and Abraham match was acceptable. It was time for the young couple to meet.

Abraham was overjoyed at being considered a match for the lovely Rosa and wanting to make a good impression dressed in his new suit, hat and shoes. Herz introduced the couple, and Abraham must have passed muster with Rosa as well because a short time later the wedding date was set and arrangements for the wedding got under way. In 1920, Rosa and Abraham were married in a small family ceremony in Josbach, and with her small dowry she moved with her new husband into his house in Sterbfritz.

Our Aunt Toni made a reception for Mother to meet the people in the Sterbfritz Jewish community, and Mother, with her charm and wit, was an immediate hit. The couple was warmly accepted, and Rosa Schuster became popular with both Sterbfritz' Christian and Jewish community members.

Rosa had a natural way with people. She had always been an outgoing girl, an extrovert they say. But more than just possessing a likable personality, Rosa was blessed with an ability that transformed her from a shopkeeper and homemaker into a peacemaker and mediator. She would have been an asset at the League of Nations had they known of her talent, a talent that came to good use when her beloved brother, Moritz, married out of the Jewish faith—an unthinkable circumstance in the Orthodox community.

Grandfather was devastated. How could Moritz do such a thing to the family? How could he show such disrespect to the people in the Jewish community? How would his grandchildren be raised Jewishly when they had a Christian for a mother? Would Moritz be able to observe dietary laws and other important Jewish laws married to a *shiksa?* Why couldn't he find a nice Jewish girl like other

Jewish boys? There were plenty of young Jewish ladies who would jump at the chance to marry an upstanding man such as Moritz.

Grandfather thought his only recourse was to disown his son; sitting *shiva* for him, he declared him dead. (In Jewish tradition, shiva is the seven-day mourning period that begins immediately after the funeral of a loved one.) The situation was so grave it threatened to tear the family, if not the community, apart. Then Rosa came to the rescue. No one quite knows what she said to Grandfather; no one will ever know. But using her special gift of persuasion, she convinced him to accept the marriage—peacefully and without rancor. Crisis averted.

Then there was the time a young Jewish woman in the town got pregnant by one of the local Jewish men, and a baby girl was soon born out of wedlock. When the child's father refused to accept responsibility, Mother mediated and convinced the young man to marry the woman he had impregnated. Again, no one knows what she said, but the couple got married, and in the end, both the husband and wife were happy. The marriage lasted their lifetime.

Rosa's kindness was unbounded. A neighbor's illness (whether Christian or Jewish) triggered an immediate visit to see how she could help. Any crisis she heard about made her spring into action offering aid. If the woman of a household took ill, Mother was the first to prepare the family meals until the lady of the house was able to do for herself. If anyone in a neighbor's family took ill, Mother was first on the scene with a pot of chicken soup. When neighbors, many illiterate, needed a letter written, they came to Mother to compose and write it for them. Our mother was a natural leader and everyone's darling wherever she went. Maybe it was her kindness. Or, maybe it was her delightful sense of humor that caused people to go helpless with laughter. Everyone loved her because she was joy itself.

On the practical side, Mother worked hard and was an exceptional housekeeper; organization was her middle name. If one could look into her linen closet or chest of drawers, the linens, towels and garments were lined up like soldiers, all in neat stacks and tied with pretty-colored ribbons. Mother was proud that her laundry was the best and cleanest in town. Laundry day meant that the large wash kettle was fired up and the water brought to a rolling boil. Mother, Bertel and Margot spent most of the day in the basement laundry room sweating over the scrub table. The result was the cleanest, whitest clothes in town, a fact that did not go unnoticed by other Sterbfritz women.

In addition to her superb housekeeping skills, Mother was extremely articulate and was able to use her verbal gifts to influence others to adopt her opinions, opinions which, unsurprisingly, held a great deal of weight with many people—none more than her own daughters, Bertel and Margot. Many teenagers, even then, displayed a certain amount of rebelliousness. Margot and Bertel did not. Both girls respected Mother to the point that when she spoke, no argument was heard.

While both girls were bright, Bertel especially excelled in her studies. She was always No.1 scholastically at any school she attended and always ended the school year with a report card loaded with A-pluses in all subjects. Even in the public school where she went after the Jewish School was closed, Lehrer Staubitz, the upper-class teacher, held Bertel up as an example to the other students. "Why can't you be as smart as that Jewish girl?" he'd ask, referring to Bertel, which embarrassed her no end, at the same time pleasing her equally as much.

Sister Margot, a year-and-a-half younger than Bertel, was equally smart, but the family joked that she didn't apply herself as did Bertel. As a result, her grades were all As, not A pluses. Poor Margot.

Years later, Rosa became a devoted and loving mother and cherished doing things that would please us and make us laugh. In the spring, our biggest joy was lambing, the time when the lambs were born, most often while in our large yard. One lambing season when I was 4 or 5 years old, my mother gave me a sweet gift. She brought a day-old lamb from the yard and carried it upstairs to my bedroom while I slept. Placing it gently on top of me, the lamb's weight brought me around. As my eyes focused, I could see the newborn lamb and hear its soft bleating. Running my fingers across his head and back, I was enchanted by its softness and cuddled it to my chest. I loved it instantly.

Another time, she brought me a newborn chick and also put it in bed with me. Again, its peeping woke me from a deep sleep, and I giggled and giggled while it cheeped and hopped around the covers and pillow. Mother looked for kind things to do for her children, and I loved her because of it.

My family was diverse. Margot, her face was full of freckles, was the tomboy of the family in addition to being a free spirit and an independent thinker. She feared nothing, and it was not unusual for her to come up the winner when she wrestled the boys her age or older. Much to their embarrassment and dismay, a tussle with Margot resulted in black eyes and bloody noses while Margot always came without a scratch. I loved Margot; she was my protector. I idolized her and wanted to be tough just like she was.

Bertel was the domestic one with a maternal instinct that spilled over onto me. When I was born, Bertel was 5 years old and instantly became my second momma, dressing me and carrying me around as if I were a doll. When Bertel developed a hernia, everyone attributed her condition to her carrying me around on her hip at that very early age. Or, maybe she was born with it. No one will ever know, but for years I felt responsible and guilty for causing her problem.

The girls learned well from Mother and the house would be well taken care of and I would be looked after with tenderness and care whenever she had to leave to visit family or take care of someone who needed her. Barely teenagers, the girls took over her domestic duties and saw to the cooking, cleaning and everything else Mother did daily. Our home was warm and caring and with Mother at the helm it also ran like a well-oiled machine.

CHAPTER
THREE

Religion and Jewish tradition were serious business for most European Jews the majority of whom were Orthodox and adhered to Jewish laws and customs in the strictest sense. In the Schuster household, my mother was the observant one while my father went along with "all that folderol" to keep the peace. My father wasn't a follower of any organized religion, Jewish or otherwise. There was just so much religion he could take, and in spite of my mother he laid down the law and refused to observe the Jewish tradition of morning and evening synagogue attendance. He did, however, agree to attend synagogue services at least on Saturday morning—the Jewish Sabbath.

Those who observed Jewish law would apply phylacteries (*tefillin* in Hebrew), which are two small leather boxes attached to leather straps worn during morning prayers by Orthodox and Conservative Jewish males over the age of 13. I only vaguely remember the few times I saw my father strap them on his arm and forehead. He did, however, observe the tradition of not doing business on Saturday, and the grocery store was closed from sundown Friday through sundown on Saturday. It was the custom to wait until three stars appeared in the sky to know if the Sabbath was over. True to form, my father needed only one star to indicate the conclusion of the Sabbath. One star and the store's doors would open.

Because my mother was ritually observant, she was required to make preparation in anticipation of the Sabbath since all forms of work, lifting, carrying, turning on lights or lighting a fire or gas stove was forbidden. Like many Jewish households, we had a live-in maid who was not Jewish and whose duty it was to light the fire in our heating stoves as well as the cook stove. She would also turn all lights on and off as required. In later years when we no longer had a maid, our neighbor, Lisel Schreiber, was engaged as our "Shabbos goy" (a Jewish expression meaning Sabbath helper who is not Jewish) who performed these chores. Though Christians may have thought our customs strange, it was never hard to find a Christian neighbor to fulfill the Shabbos goy duties. They were paid well for their efforts, and it took them very little time to perform basic household duties. Once done, the Sabbath helper could return home to her own family.

Our synagogue was built in the late 18th century, not an ornate structure as in wealthier big-city synagogues, but solid and well built. Only men and boys were permitted to worship on the first floor, as was tradition. Women who attended services were seated in the balcony, and if the synagogue was so small that there was no balcony, the first floor was divided between the men's side and the women's side, and a visual barrier was placed between. The rabbis, wise men that they are, were aware how the sight of a pretty ankle or the curve of a soft pink cheek could break all concentration on prayer. Flirting could be done before or after services. Services were a time to think about God.

While some have criticized the Jewish faith as being sexist because women aren't allowed to read the Torah during services, are not required to say prayers at specified times of the day and are separated from the men in services, my opinion is that Judaism is preferential to women. Judaism recognizes the difficulty of rearing children, preparing meals, sewing clothes, knitting socks, mufflers and mittens as well as keeping the fires lit and the house neat and tidy. With such a heavy responsibility, why would God require a woman to drop what she is doing to say a prayer? In Judaism, a woman's life is a prayer. God requires nothing more from her.

In the Sterbfritz synagogue, the seating capacity on the lower floor was approximately 100 men and 20 to 30 boys. It was further divided by the boy's section in the front on the right side of the *hazzan* (prayer leader) who was, in most cases, also the Jewish teacher. Boys being boys, even pious Jewish boys, the location of the boy's section was intentional. The cantor/teacher could see the boys at all times and immediately nip any potential horseplay in the bud with a stern look or a sharp cough. Fearing the worst kind of punishment, we were nearly always on our best behavior.

The balcony, where my mother and sisters sat, was accessible only from the second floor, and in Germany all seats were arranged so that congregants faced east toward the Holy Land. At the very front of the room was the Holy Ark that contained the scriptures (Torah) and immediately in front of the Ark was the lectern from which the cantor sang and led the congregation in prayer. In the center of the edifice was the *bemah*, a lectern-like structure large enough to hold the huge Torah scroll, and where the scriptures were read aloud to the congregants.

My father sat in a pew nearest the front on the left side, and I don't remember seeing anyone else sit with him. On either side of the bemah were the seats of the congregation's president and vice president, my Uncle Moritz Schuster being the vice president during my entire life in Sterbfritz. Pews were purchased in those days, and the wealthier the congregant the higher the dues and the nearer to the bemah he sat. Religious, but very poor congregants like Lazarus Hecht, could not afford to pay high dues, so they sat all the way in the rear.

The only Christian church in Sterbfritz, the Lutheran church, was a stone's throw from my house, and while I never knew just what going to church was all about, I figured it was pretty much like going to synagogue—only on Sunday instead of Saturday. But while many of my friends were Christian, *being* Christian was nothing more remarkable to me than a person's height, weight or hair color. Some things just were, and we didn't question them. But the church, as well as the minister, were a puzzlement, and because we didn't understand, we kept our distance on Sunday mornings as we watched the *Pfarrer* (Lutheran minister), dressed in his long black robe with miter in hand, walk from the rectory to the church, as the bell tower came alive with the sonorous peal of bells.

As I got older, my friends and I were no longer intimidated by the Pfarrer, and as congregants filed into the church, we sneaked over the fence from Uncle Moritz' rear garden into the minister's yard. There, we positioned ourselves in front of his turkey pen and gobbled loudly to make the turkeys gobble back. Invariably, it created a racket that could not only be heard inside the church, it drowned out the minister's preaching as well. Our prank ended soon when the minister caught us and boxed our ears.

I think I inherited my sense of ease with people from my father, and in my world that meant being at ease with Christians as well as Jews. In my unsophisticated mind, everybody was a friend, and especially good friends were Wilhelm and Klaus Koleb, gentile brothers about my age who lived directly across the street.

Wilhelm and Klaus were just two kids in a family of 12, but because these two boys and I were the same age we became fast friends and did what boys did to entertain themselves—things like scavenging for worn-out wagon wheels to salvage the rims. It was always a grand day spent rolling wheel rims down the streets. Keeping a rim rolling without wobbling and falling over was a bit of a trick, but after many attempts I was finally able to master the skill and rev it up with a stick just before it veered off into the gutter.

When we tired of that, there was always a rousing game of marbles. I supplied the marbles because Klaus and Wilhelm's father couldn't afford to spend money on unessential things like marbles. We played in a circle drawn in the dirt, and it was a game at which my sister Bertel excelled. Wilhelm, Klaus and I often teamed up to beat her, but she was a better player, and we almost always ended up losing all our marbles to her.

Collecting her winnings in her skirt, she ended further play by taking them to her room and emptying the marbles over the surface of the bed. Holding each pretty glass orb to the light, she cherished each one. We couldn't play again until she had admired them all and categorized each by size or color, kept the ones she liked best and put the rest back into play.

In comparison to the Kolebs, my family was well off, a fact I didn't fully appreciate until I was older. I was aware, however, that I had more toys and better clothes and shoes. But, I was happy to share just to be in their company. We flew kites, kicked a soccer ball that I got from my cousin, Alfred, who was the best soccer player Sterbfritz had ever produced, and went ice skating—alternating who would wear the skates. Then there was hide-and-seek, riding my scooter and walking on stilts—the one toy the Kolebs could provide because it was handmade by Mr. Koleb. Bored with all that, we held peeing contests to see who could pee the farthest, a game that Klaus, being the oldest and having the biggest, always won.

Kasper Koleb, Wilhelm and Klaus' father, was barely able to make enough money to provide for his large brood. His wife, Minna, a haggard-looking woman, seemed always in poor health, maybe from giving birth to so many children. She could do no more than a few of the household basics, and my mother was often at her house offering to help when she felt the worst or when she had just had another child, which was often.

I don't remember what Kasper Koleb did for a living to shelter, feed and clothe all his family members. I only remember he supplemented his meager income with part-time work and had a makeshift lumberyard behind his house. He had an electric saw, I remember, with which he cut logs into firewood-sized pieces for his customers, including the Schusters. In those days, logs could be purchased from foresters who would then deliver them to Kasper to cut into smaller pieces. Once cut into a manageable size, they were further chopped into smaller pieces that would fit into stoves and ovens. Long before central heating, the kitchen stove and oven were the only heat anyone had. Kasper's logs served as fuel for cooking year 'round and for heating in the winter.

Later, my parents would supplement the firewood with coal briquettes, which burned longer and hotter and left less ash to be carried to the ash pile. It also took less space. The firewood was stored in the woodshed and took up the entire shed, whereas the coal was kept in a coal bin in the basement that left room for storage of other things.

Next door to Kasper lived his brother George, George's wife and three daughters. The oldest girl was my sister Bertel's age, and they spent hours sharing secrets, giggling, and doing what girls that age do. Both Koleb families were stretched financially and raised pigs not only for food for the family but to sell to supplement their meager income. With so many people in the two households, you'd think some family member would have been recruited to herd the pigs to their daily forage. It surprises me that they spent the money to pay the pig herder, Mack, to herd their pigs to the fields. But every morning, their pigs joined the others for a blissful day in the municipal corral's mud.

CHAPTER
FOUR

On January 30, 1933, Adolf Hitler was appointed German chancellor by President Paul von Hindenburg, and the appointment marked Hitler's first step toward complete control of the government and his aim to turn Germany into a police state. From 1933 to 1939, Hitler continued to build his weapons arsenal, but ironically didn't need it to gobble up neighboring Austria and Czechoslovakia because both countries surrendered without a fight. Next, Hitler took aim at Poland, another easy prey, and in September 1939, German troops crossed the Polish border. Forewarned that a Polish or Romanian invasion would force Britain and France to declare war, Germany thumbed its nose at both countries and World War II began.

Inside Germany, Hitler geared up for Jewish extermination. Testing the waters by removing Jewish rights little by little, one by one, Hitler was able to determine how far the German people would allow him to go. As Jews were robbed of their possessions and ability to support themselves, German gentiles were simultaneously rewarded for anti-Semitic acts with medals and recognition by Der Führer himself. When the Jews were rounded up and sent to concentration camps, good *Germans uttered not a peep.*

I remember that in early 1933 things began to change rapidly, especially in small towns like Sterbfritz. Before the spring of 1933, the German government subsidized all parochial schools, but one of the first acts the Nazis instituted was subsidizing all schools *but* the Jewish schools. The Jewish community in Sterbfritz, being made up mostly of financially strapped families, was not able to pay teachers even if a schoolroom could have been requisitioned. Consequently, the Jewish school soon closed as did many Jewish schools all over Germany. All eight grades from the Jüdische Schule were transferred to the public school, the Volkschule, under the tutelage of one Fräulein Meyers, a small, pretty woman with golden highlights in her long brown hair, which she wore in one heavy braid down her back. Fräulein Meyers taught first, second and third grades. She was kind, but strict, and kept complete order in the classroom. Jewish or Christian, she treated all students fairly. We were particularly grateful when she excused the Jewish kids from the mandatory Christian religion classes. A kindly soul, I'm sure her superiors would not have approved had they known.

But despite Fräulein Meyers' kindness, there was a snag. The school session in the Volkschule began on Monday and ended on Saturday, and Saturday was Shabbat, the Jewish Sabbath. In Jewish Orthodoxy, no one is allowed to work on the Sabbath and writing lessons was considered work. When we attended the Jewish school, classes were never held on Saturday, and the lost time was made up by holding classes on Sundays.

Wonderful Fräulein Meyers took it upon herself to make sure that while we were compelled to attend classes on Saturday we would not be required to write. All writing assignments were postponed until Sunday when the school was closed. Lessons completed on Sunday were submitted and graded on Monday morning.

Except for Saturday classes, the schedule at the Volkschule didn't interfere with Jewish tradition. The day started at 7 a.m., and classes went until noon. After a lunch at home, all Jewish students attended Lehrer (teacher) Georg Friess' Hebrew classes from 2 until 4 p.m.

Friess was a young Jewish man in his early twenties who was compensated, along with his salary, by getting free room and board at one of the student's homes; during this time it was at the home of Elsie and Jacob Hecht. Circumstances compelled the Hechts to take in this boarder because Jacob, a horse dealer, had fallen on hard times and needed the money. They welcomed this energetic, handsome and athletic young man into their household, and more so the money he brought with him.

Adventuresome, Friess stunned Sterbfritz by arriving in town on a motorcycle in a blue haze of gasoline exhaust, a fact that didn't endear him to the staid pillars of the community but impressed the heck out of us kids. It must have impressed Elsie Hecht as well because before long there were rumors that all was not strictly kosher in the Hecht household. There was a great deal of whispering among the adults, and even we kids got wind that something was amiss. Eventually, everyone found out that Friess was having an affair with Elsie Hecht, and the whole town seemed to know about it except the cuckolded husband. Perhaps he did know and felt it better to ignore his wife's indescretions. As I said, times were hard, and they needed the money.

His private life, however, did not diminish Lehrer Friess' ability to teach and keep control of his classroom. Friess was a strict disciplinarian and believed in corporal punishment, but because we respected him we rarely stepped out of line. On the rare occasion that a boy got too rowdy, the Friess spanking stick was never far from his hand. More often than not, his punishments were benign. Once, when we boys got overly rambunctious, he assigned us to write: "We promise to be better behaved." a thousand times. Giving us a week to accomplish the task, my mother and sisters, sympathizing with my plight, disguised their handwriting to look like mine and wrote most of the sentences for me. All in all, they wrote more than half, and Friess must not have checked it too thoroughly as he was satisfied with the results.

In addition to teaching Hebrew, Friess was a cantor. The district rabbi, Rabiner Horowitz of Hanau, disapproved of Friess, interestingly not because of the Elsie Hecht business, but because Friess' father wasn't Jewish. But there was little he could do to prevent Friess from being a cantor at services or teaching Hebrew after school because his mother was Jewish, and according to Jewish law, if your mother is Jewish, you are Jewish. End of story.

Living in Sterbfritz was getting harder and harder for all Jews, and I think it was the hardest for Jewish children. In April of 1935, I was transferred from Miss Meyer's class to Lehrer Weidling's class. Prior to 1933, Lehrer Weidling felt comfortable to associate with Jews and was often in our company playing cards on a Sunday afternoon at Michel Schuster's café. But in 1934, he, like many others, joined the Nazi party. Abruptly, his attitude changed. Heretofore a congenial man with a smile and a good word for everyone, he now became hostile and belligerent to his former Jewish friends. The transformation was startling.

He was probably a cruel man all along, his meanness purposely hidden, but hidden so well we never suspected. I remember that before he showed animosity toward Jews, he relished killing squirrels with his shotgun, enjoying immensely the sight of blood dripping from the squirrels' mangled bodies as he held each one up to admire.

Humiliation was his forte, and he was a master at humiliating Jewish youngsters. In the classroom, he manifested his Jewish enmity and increased his status with the local Nazis by goading the gentile kids into tormenting Jewish kids. One of his favorite debasements was to force Jewish kids to sing anti-Jewish hate songs, hoping we would learn to loathe ourselves as much as he loathed us.

Once, Weidling singled me out and demanded I sing the "Horst Wessel" anti-Jewish hate song, solo, in front of the whole class. I don't now remember all the words, perhaps I just don't want to remember, but I do recall the part where the lyrics were about good Germans rolling Jewish heads down the street. I knew all the words then, I had heard them sung a hundred times. Hating the song, I insisted that I didn't know it. Still, he demanded I start singing, and as I stumbled over the words and fought back tears, he shouted in my face, humiliating me by calling me a "stupid Jew."

I don't know how I mustered the courage, but when he called me a stupid Jew in front of the whole class I rebelled and refused to sing even one more note. I was a tough little kid, and at that point, nothing or no one could make me sing that ugly song even as he punished me by painfully cracking my palms with his switch, an 18-inch wooden instrument he reserved for just for punishing Jews. Dressed down and whipped for nothing in front of the whole class, I never wanted to go back. There was not a day I didn't get a whipping from him for rule infractions that changed daily, while the gentile kids looked on and laughed. He looked for any excuse to hand out punishment for offences both real and imagined, and Lehrer Weidling's persecution gave license to the other kids to torment us as well. Emulating the teacher's behavior, we were hit, cursed and called names by gentile kids on our way home from school. They called us "dirty Jew," "smelly Jew" or "pig Jew." Often, they threw rocks at me, and I can still feel the pain when they met their mark. Bigger kids than me lay in wait, knocking me down and beating me until I was bloody. My former so-called friends, the Kolebs, turned on me as well and were among the most vicious. Joining the Hitler Youth gave them, for the first time in their lives, a status they had never had before, and they were the first to throw rocks hidden in snowballs. Once, when the Kolebs threw snowballs with rocks, they nearly knocked me out. I thought I was going to pass out, and when my vision cleared, I saw the snow around me was bloodied.

Even Frau Koleb turned on my mother, forgetting how Mother had fixed meals for her family when she was sick or laid up with one more pregnancy. The Nazi government gave Frau Koleb a status she had never known before by bestowing a special award on her for having produced 12 children, an award that was signed by Hitler himself. For the first time, Frau Koleb felt better than the Schusters, and the shame of years of poverty manifested itself in lashing out in the worst way against what they must have felt were their former betters.

Not only was I tormented, my sisters felt the ugliness of anti-Semitism at school as well. As part of the school curriculum, all upper-grade girls had to attend sewing and knitting classes conducted by a spinster named Frau Schotte. Frau Schotte was also the local piano teacher, and like most non-Jews, was an ardent Nazi. As part of the school curriculum, my sisters were required to go to class in her house and study home economics, part of which was learning stitchery. Enjoying the sense of power afforded by state-sanctioned anti-Semitism, Frau Schotte encouraged her gentile students to aggrieve the Jewish girls, turning her back on verbal attacks and occasional punches or slaps. Pathologically mean, she occasionally stuck the Jewish girls with her knitting needles, sometimes drawing blood.

Frau Schotte was well known for having a kennel with six or seven large dogs whose personalities were as vicious as her own. The German shepherds were evil incarnate, snarling and clawing at the chain link fence whenever anyone passed, trying to find an escape route so they could attack. Often, they snarled at my sisters and me whe we passed. There was no way to avoid passing her house to get to where our Tante Rosa, Milan, Mina, Norbert and Ina lived. Passing the Schotte residence, the dogs, fangs exposed and saliva flying, were frustrated at not being able to get to their prey. But as bad luck would have it, one day one of her dogs escaped the kennel. With a snarl, it took off after me and quickly overtook me, his teeth sunk in my buttocks and my flesh and pants were torn. Fortunately, my cousin Norbert saw the dog, shouted and waved his arms desperately trying to scare him off. Sobbing, I clung to Norbert's legs, hoping the dog would go away. At her window, peeking out from behind lace curtains, Frau Schotte saw the commotion but merely stared, ignoring the attack. My cousin saved my life because I'm sure the dog, who weighed only a little less than I did, would have killed me if it had not been stopped.

Fear reigned and not only in the school and not only among the Jews. Any gentile found aiding or comforting a Jew was held suspect. Multiple offenses warranted ostracism, and the label "Jew lover," and it wasn't long before Lisel Schreiber, our Shabbos goy, was afraid to come to our house to perform her Shabbat chores. Nervously apologizing, she backed out of the doorway into the street, with excuse after excuse, tears filling her eyes. My mother was left standing in the doorway, unable to utter a word. There were no words that could explain what was happening to our world.

An optimist at heart, I took the whole Lisel Schreiber thing in stride and figured there had to be a way around this Shabbos predicament. Turning on lights during the Sabbath was forbidden, but there had to be a way to turn them on and still keep the laws. It was easy! Since German light switches worked on a rotary system, that is you turned a knob instead of flipping a switch, I attached a string to a piece of wood that fit over the switch, set a large alarm clock on the floor and weighted the clock so it to would remain solidly on the floor. Then, I attached the string to the alarm clock's ringer key and set the alarm clock to go off at the prescribed time.

When the clock rang, the windup key turned and wound the string around its stem. Slowly, slowly, the light switch turned until, voilá, it was in the off position. This was a feat that earned me the reputation of being a genius, an elevated status I enjoyed immensely.

On August 2, 1934, President von Hindenberg died giving Adolf Hitler the ability to gain even more power and government control by combining the office of president and chancellor and assuming the title of Führer. He also increased the number of men in the SA (Sturmabteilung, a military organization that aided Hitler in his rise to power) to 2.5 million, 25 times the number of men assigned to the regular army.

In early 1934, a very young man by the name of Müller arrived in Sterbfritz from a larger community. He was to assume the position of the Sterbfritz new Bürgermeister (mayor). He was an ardent anti-Semite, and his appointment was made directly by Reichsmarschall Hermann Göring, Hitler's No. 3 man in the Nazi government.

Being in the right place at the right time, Göring met Müller while he and his party were on a hunting trip approximately 30 kilometers from Sterbfritz. While staying at the Gasthaus Müller in Jossa, young Müller was called upon to be their hunting guide and weapons carrier. Göring was so pleased with Müller's services, taking them to the best hunting spots where they were able to bag as many deer as they could shoot, he presented him with a Golden Hakenkreuz (swastika) and arranged for him to be the mayor of Sterbfritz. To receive a Golden Swastika was the highest honor the Nazi party could bestow.

Immediately upon Müller's arrival, one of his first official acts was to organize the Sturm Abteilung, also referred to as the S.A. and better known as the Brown Shirts. They were called Brown Shirts because they actually wore brown shirts with red and black swastika armbands. Once initiated, they swore allegiance to the Nazi Party and Adolf Hitler. With the arrival of the Brown Shirts, life in Sterbfritz changed drastically. Müller, assuming even more authority over time, was awarded money from the central government to subsidize the S.A. into an ever-stronger presence in addition to organizing a Sterbfritz chapter of the Hitler Jugend (Hitler Youth). To my knowledge, all of Sterbfritz' young people who were not of Jewish heritage joined the Hitler Youth; my friends Wilhelm and Klaus Koleb were among the first to sign up.

Life became more and more constricted as more and more restrictions were placed on Jews both economically and socially. Our family, once prosperous because of my parent's industriousness, was now just scraping by. Because of a national edict, Germans were not allowed to buy from Jewish merchants, and consequently my parent's family business suffered. Not only did our grocery business decline but Father's travels had to be curtailed. Many loyal customers were afraid to do business with him—a dirty Jew. Sales fell to nothing, and to his dismay it wasn't long before there was no money coming in to care for his family. To survive, he was forced to sell everything but life's essentials. His beloved horse, Frieda, and our pretty little buggy went to the highest bidder. He kept the cow, however, needing it for milk and cheese. A cow, at this point, was worth more than its weight in gold because it was used not only for the milk it provided but it was also used to pull the plow. Hitched together with Cousin Norbert's cow, the two animals were the sole beasts of burden used to cultivate the fields, a circumstance not unusual for cows at the time. Often, farmers who could not afford horses used dairy cows as beasts of burden.

In addition, the grocery store business fell off as well so my father looked for a buyer and was fortunate to find one—a man by the name of Herr Kirst. An amiable man, Kirst agreed not only to make monthly payments toward the purchase but to pay rent for the store as well. My father thought it was a blessing from God.

Not alone in our predicament, all German-Jewish families fell on hard times. Sterbfritz Jews in the cattle business *(Viehändler)* traditionally traded their cattle in Steinau at the cattle mart. But the government decrees that restricted the grocery business also affected the cattle dealers, and they found that an immediate solution was to sell all their assets to non-Jews. (Interestingly, in our part of Germany, Jews dominated the cattle business. Consequently, all transactions by Jews and non-Jews were accomplished with Hebrew numbers. Even after Jews could no longer participate at the market, the sales were still transacted in Hebrew.)

Money was so scarce my parents had sell store items on credit. The 1935 Nüremberg edict decreed that non-Jews were no longer required to pay their debts to Jews. Now, not only were non-Jews forbidden to do business with Jews, they were also exempt from paying prior debts. Overhearing my parent's kitchen conversations, I learned that our accounts receivables were in the thousands. And while Jews were still required to pay their debts, because other Jews had as little money as my parents, there was no money coming in. The situation was dire. Somehow, Father was able scrape together enough money to pay the monthly mortgage payments to the bank in Schlüchtern. He was also able to keep up the payments on a small Italian life insurance policy he had purchased years before. Somehow, we managed.

So many of my mother's beautiful things had to be sold. Anything that was not absolutely necessary to survive had to go. Her prized linens, washed and starched, the bundles tied with pink ribbons, were the first to be sold. Anything that would bring a price was put up or sale—even my dog, Fritzi, a dachshund I loved with all my heart, had to be sold to raise money for food. I didn't know what would become of my dog if I weren't there to protect him, feed him and scratch his ears. My whole world was turned upside down, and I couldn't stop crying. Father tried to dry my tears, but they kept coming.

I don't know who bought my dog; I didn't ask. But one day he was just gone. To pacify me, Father promised to buy me a wagon as a replacement for the dog, but we both knew it wasn't true. Wagons were as unessential as dachshunds.

Still, we country Jews were more fortunate than Jews who lived in the cities. We still had the land, and with sweat and muscle it produced enough food to keep us alive—vegetables from the garden and fruit from the orchard. We still managed to have food on the table daily.

Never having experienced the discrimination and deep anti-Jewish hatred that seemed to build every day, Jews could only hope it was temporary. If they accepted the indignities, went along, surely Germany would come to its senses and everything would return to normal. Our father, devastated by what was happening to his Sterbfritz, could not understand any of it. He was a respected, hardworking man. Our tormentors were people we had known and liked all our lives. Why, now, did they hate us so much?

My parents hid their fear, never letting their children know the dept of their despair and concern. They kept our home life as normal as possible, encouraging us to be good children and do our best in school and at home. Despite the dangers we faced outside our front door, we were a strong family. We always felt the love our parents had for us. Mother especially, the wonderful person that she was, made sure she kept our spirits high, and that we all made the best of the situation.

But hate and fear came to our doorstep. Late one night, a Hitler Youth mob gathered in front of Uncle Moritz Schuster's house, which was next door to ours. We hid in my bedroom, which faced

Uncle Moritz' house, and listened to their ugly anti-Semitic hate songs. Irritated because they were not getting a response from their victims, one of the thugs threw a rock that missed Uncle Moritz' house but sailed through my bedroom window, crashing through the glass pane. Shattered glass flew everywhere, and the rock barely missed my sister Bertel. Enraged, Father wanted to confront the mob, but we feared he would be killed and begged him not to go; Mother was able to stop him before he could get to the door. We lived through the night but the stress took its toll. Not long after, Father was dead.

CHAPTER
FIVE

In 1935, the Nuremberg Laws, laws that removed all Jewish civil rights in addition to revoking Jewish citizenship, were put into effect. For the first time in history, discrimination was based on race and ancestry, not religious beliefs, and many nonpracticing as well as observant Jews were stripped of their rights as well as their ability to earn a living. The 120 laws that comprised the Nuremberg Laws also made it unlawful for gentiles to marry or have sexual relations with a person of Jewish descent. Common social intercourse with a Jew was also forbidden. In addition, no Jew was allowed to have a radio and reading newspapers was forbidden to Jews.

My father was our rock. From him, our family got its strength. His gigantic size and booming voice demanded attention and respect, and it was given to him. Not subject to random illness, his childhood bout with typhus affected his ability to walk normally but seemed to gird him against further sickness. Strong and proud, the pain in his legs and feet was constant, but only a nuisance. He'd often joke that if his feet were as good as his heart, he would be a happy man. Ironically, it was his heart that most likely caused his premature death.

On Friday May 5, 1935, Abraham Schuster visited many of his Jewish friends and jokingly said, "If I don't see you again, let me wish you a good Sabbath." Returning home around lunchtime, he kicked off his heavy, mud-caked boots and left them outside the kitchen door. In stocking feet, he lumbered to the kitchen table where he sat in his favorite chair and relaxed while my mother and Bertel fixed lunch. With lunch only half eaten, he suddenly moaned as if in great pain. His whole body went limp, and in a second or two he slowly slid to the floor.

Bertel rushed to fetch Dr. Boot, our family doctor, but he could not, or would not, leave his house to attend my father. Dr. Boot, along with all other Christian doctors, was not allowed to care for Jewish patients. Seeing that nothing would be done for our father, Bertel ran to the school building to get Margot and me. But, it was too late. Father was already dead and had probably died instantly from either a cerebral hemorrhage or a heart attack. We found our mother on the floor with him, rocking her beloved husband in her arms like a baby. Her disconsolate sobbing could be heard on the street, but no neighbors came to help.

With little money to spend on a casket, several Jewish men garnered enough lumber from Kalmann Schuster's factory to hurriedly build a simple coffin. Jewish Law dictates that the dead be buried before the following sundown and in the plainest of wooden boxes. But this was the Sabbath. Jewish Law also forbids burying the dead on this holy day. My father's burial, therefore, was postponed until Sunday afternoon.

Our community of German Jews observed the Jewish Laws and father's body was attended by male members of the *chevra kadisha*, that is, those who had been trained to prepare the body for burial. His body was washed then dressed in a white shroud and placed in the wooden coffin.

I desperately wanted to see him. I couldn't believe he was gone. That I would never walk with him, never feel the safety of his presence ever again was unfathomable. When at last I was allowed to enter the room in which he had been placed, I could just barely see his face over the rim of the wooden coffin. He was pale, but peaceful looking, as if he were only sleeping. My chest constricted, I willed with all my might that he would sit up, laugh in his booming voice and tell me it was all a joke. But it wasn't. My father would never hug me again. Never tell me the things a boy needs his father to tell him. For the first time in my life, standing in a room full of people, I felt totally alone, experiencing my first taste from life's bitter cup.

The next minute, a man named Jakob took my reluctant hands, and insisted that I place them on my father's ankles. He told me to repeat a prayer that he read to me while I did so. A terrible feeling came over me. My father was cold. His skin felt like wax. This was not my father, the man I loved so dearly, but a waxen image. In spite of my revulsion, I obediently repeated the prayer, and when it was finished I quickly fled from the room.

The Jewish cemetery in Altengronau was shared by Jews from Sterbfritz and several other surrounding communities, and it was approximately two-and-a-half miles from Sterbfritz. In the 15th century, as Jews came from the cities to settle in villages, they were granted a parcel of land on top of a mountain at the edge of Altengronau for burying their dead. The road to the cemetery was dirt, steep and narrow, and it often took several horses and the help of several men pushing to get coffins to the top.

One of my father's relatives, a horse dealer, was miraculously able to retain several horses from his business, so his team was hitched to a wagon and the coffin placed in the wagon bed. The funeral procession began. As a child, I couldn't know the impact my father had on so many people. Nor could I know how many people he had helped and the depth of their own sorrow at his death. What I saw surprised and amazed me, for when I looked down the hill behind me, I saw hundreds of non-Jews who put their lives in peril to honor a man they loved. Though they stayed 500 feet behind the processional and stopped at the town limits, they had come to honor my father with their presence when he went to his final rest.

Our grieving mother, Bertel, Margot and I walked behind the makeshift hearse all the way to the cemetery. Lacking a rabbi, Lehrer Friess conducted the services and our father's first cousin delivered the eulogy.

Returning from home the cemetery, shiva began. Jewish tradition requires mourners to wear slippers and sit on low stools or pillows in their house for seven days while friends and neighbors drop by to pay their respects. For the first 30 days of mourning, one wears a rent garment, a lapel or sleeve that is purposely torn to show grief. Men are prohibited from shaving or cutting their hair, and daily prayers are said in the home. Sitting shiva, as it is called, lasts until the next Sabbath eve. I don't remember much about the mourning period except there were always lots of people coming and going and a lot of praying. I remember the Jewish women bringing baskets of food.

My world was shaken by my father's death, and immediately after the funeral I had an allergy attack that made my left arm swell to twice its normal size. It lasted for the entire mourning period, but when it was over, my arm miraculously returned to normalcy. With no one else to turn to, Uncle Moritz now acted as my surrogate father. He took me to synagogue services early every morning and every evening, where, per Jewish tradition, I recited Kaddish for my father for the next 11 months.

My father's death left my mother alone to run the household and conclude what she could of my father's business dealings. Now, no money came into our home that was not earned by my mother's hand because my father's investments with gentiles were canceled by the government. With jobs as scarce as they were for Jews, Jewish debts went into default. My father had co-signed a note for his friend, Abraham Goldschmidt, but he died shortly before the note was due. Goldschmidt, not having the means to repay the loan, looked to my mother to pay. When she could not come up with the money either, the note holder confiscated the proceeds from our father's life insurance policy, shattering what meager financial prospects we might have had.

That summer, to earn money to support us, Mother, Bertel and Margot got jobs as laundresses at the Hotel Strauss in Bad Brückenau, a spa town with numerous hotels and mineral baths that catered to a wealthy clientele. Two of those hotels were kosher, frequented by wealthy Jews whose money and position, until then, had miraculously shielded them from governmental decrees. In 1935, these hotels were still allowed to exist, and Mother and the girls were given a room on the employee's floor. Room and board were provided, and with no expenses they were able to save all the money they earned.

Because Mother was not allowed to have a small child at the hotel, I was sent to a summer camp/children's home in Bad Kissingen, a spa town about 15 miles to the northeast of Bad Brückenau. Bad Kissingen was larger than Brückenau, and its hotels and resorts catered to an even more affluent clientele. The town, known the world over for its sulfur hot springs, attracted people from all over Germany for the so-called healing power of the sulfur baths and mudpacks.

The first few days I was at the camp were hardest in my young life. Emotionally, I was devastated. My father recently dead, my mother and sisters living what seemed like a world away, I cried myself to sleep, and it was all I could do to pull myself together during the day. Everything I had known and loved was ripped from me. Reverting to a younger safer time, I started to suck my thumb again, something the other kids found hilarious, teasing me until I cried. It seemed like I was always crying.

But the good part was that I was among Jews, and that summer I was at least safe from anti-Semitism. After the first week, I relaxed, stopped crying and joined the other kids in games and activities. In fact, I remember being very happy. The best part was getting an extra cup of cocoa every afternoon, a reward given to the best-behaved camper. I always made sure I was the best-behaved camper.

But, there was one occasion when I wasn't. A bigger and older boy was jealous that I always got the cocoa prize, so he spit in my face to show his contempt for their choice of a prize recipient. As little as I was, I was a scrapper. Anger got the best of me, and I retaliated with a jab to his midsection; he returned fire with a series of punches that knocked me to the ground and the wind right out of me. Courageous as I was, he was bigger and stronger and before the camp counselor could separate us (for which I was grateful), I took a substantial beating. Unlike today, both parties in a ruckus were not routinely reprimanded. Who was the aggressor was the only issue—who started it—and I got my comeuppance when my attacker was roundly punished.

Summer over, my mother, sisters and I all converged on Sterbfritz together—they to find work, if they could, I to return to school and the cruel tutelage of Lehrer Weidling, whose viciousness had increased over the summer. I dreaded it.

Weidling's animosity toward Jews had increased, if that was possible, or he had gotten bolder, maybe both. He used his position and authority to torment all his Jewish students, but for some reason, me in particular. Still warm in September, he decided to take his classes to the local swimming pool for an outing with the intent of teaching lifesaving techniques to the upper classmen. Needing a drowning victim, he pointed at me.

"*Heinz, geh ins Wasser*," ("Heinz, go into the water.") he shouted, indicating with his hands that I should jump into the deep end of the pool. Not knowing how to swim, I refused and moved away from the water's edge. Angered by my refusal, he grabbed my arm and pulled me toward the edge, and reaching it he gave me a nasty shove that sent me screaming and flailing into the water. I tried to keep my head above water, but the harder I tried the more water I swallowed. Panicking, I went rigid, sank to the bottom and breathed in more water. With a real drowning victim at last, Weidling sent one of the boys to jump in and save me, but the boy wasn't strong enough to pull me out. Taking his time, Weidling found a long pole and handed it to him while two other boys jumped in and brought me to the edge of the pool. Close to being drowned, I went unconscious and I don't know what happened next. My next memory was seeing my mother's face as she bent down to comfort me. Somehow, I had been taken home and was in my own bed. The thought of going into water petrifies me to this day.

Always looking for an opportunity to inflict pain and suffering on his Jewish students, later that autumn Weidling took the class on a bird watching outing. There was a wooded area he said that had many different kinds of birds, and he took pleasure in pointing out various species to the eager young pupils. Walking back to the school, his face lit up.

"Aha! This is a perfect opportunity to give lessons in knot tying," he exclaimed. He had brought several ropes with him, which he uncoiled, and looking around pointed to my friend Hans Stern and me. He ordered us to stand next to two trees that were near us. Then he ordered the other boys to turn us upside down and hold us against the tree trunk. Uncoiling the rope, he wrapped it around us as well as the trees, making sure we were securely bound. I couldn't move, and blood was running to my head making my vision spotty. It seemed like thunder roared in my ears but it was only the sound of their voices, taunting and laughing. I could make out vicious taunts and ridicule. I screamed and tried to wriggle free but succeeded only in making the rope cut into my legs, arms and throat until they bled.

Calmly looking around at the other students, Weidling asked if anyone wanted to volunteer to untie us. Giggling, no one volunteered, while one after the other began calling us anti-Semitic names.

Joining in the laughter, Weidling shrugged his shoulders and told us that since no one wanted to untie us, we'd have to stay there. He said it would be cold that night, below freezing, he thought, and that if no one untied us we might freeze or, if in the unlikely event we made it through the night, hungry birds would peck our eyes out come morning. Dismissing the class, the laughter now raucous, everyone left us there and went home.

All, but one. Our friend and classmate, Sofi Hecht, ran to my house to get help. When she knocked on the door, Bertel answered and Sofi told her what had happened. Bertel ran to us, untied two very scared boys and calmed us down. We were hysterical from fear. Hans was so frightened he'd peed his pants. Humiliated by his wet pants' crotch, Bertel wrapped her sweater around his waist so no one would see the stain. Then, she took us home. This was only the start. From then on, every day and every place we went, we were subjected to more torture both mental and physical.

Our neighbor, Herr Recker, was one of a handful of non-Jewish neighbors who had a radio. Never missing an opportunity to humiliate Jews, my family in particular, in front of the community, he attached a speaker to a radio and placed the speaker in the open window of his house. When Hitler or Joseph Goebbels (who was the Reichsminister of public enlightenment and propaganda from 1933—1945) addressed the nation, he turned the volume up so everyone could hear. Crowds gathered outside our side-by-side houses to listen to the vile attacks against the Jews. Geared to work people into an anti-Semitic frenzy, we knew that following one of these speeches, anti-Semitic actions would flair up and we would be in trouble.

Even going to a movie was filled with torment. Because Sterbfritz, like many small towns, had no movie theater, films were shown in local businesses that had rooms big enough as well as windows that could be darkened. I saw my first movie in a tavern. Once there was a particular movie that all school children were required to see. I don't remember the name of the movie or what it was about. I only know Jews were portrayed as ugly, hateful beings, equal to pigs. Watching it, I wanted to sink into the floor and would have if it had been possible. I felt all eyes were on me, but there was no escape.

When it was over and the lights came up, everybody, including the Jewish kids, had to sing the most disgusting anti-Jewish songs. We were also forced to give the Hitler salute, "Heil, Hitler." I wished I could die.

But my problems were small compared to the suffering of the Jewish adults. For reasons unknown to us, Bürgermeister Müller felt Jews owed a debt to the community for being allowed to live there and ordered one person per Jewish family to report for work in a road gang, crushing stones that would be spread on a street that needed repair. Because there was no man in our household, mother was compelled to report. Fearing for her life and not wanting to leave her on her own, Margot and I went with her to help fulfill her duty.

Everywhere we looked, there was something ugly, something anti-Semitic that said we were worthless, less than human. The swastika, long a symbol of gentile German supremacy, was everywhere. Even the old factory with its tall, brick smokestack flew a flag with a swastika, a sight so odious that an unknown person climbed up during the night and took it down.

Immediately and without proof, Müller blamed a 20-year-old relative of ours, Ernst Schuster, but because he had no proof he couldn't arrest him. Looking for a rule infraction that he could attribute to Ernst, he finally knew if he looked hard enough he would find one. Enlisting the aid of Brown Shirts, his house was searched for illegal firearms since it was unlawful for Jews to possess them. While the Brown Shirts pretended to search the downstairs, another sneaked up the stairs to the attic and planted a rifle under a box of Passover dishes. Working their way to the attic, the discovery was made, and at long last Müller had his reason to arrest Ernst. Ernst's father, Kalmann, paid the large fine to get his son released, but Müller wasn't satisfied. With total authority to do so, he sentenced Ernst to exile, and he was mandated to leave the country at once.

Within a week, Ernst was on his way to Palestine. He didn't know it then, but he was one of the lucky ones.

In 1936, the Olympics were held in Berlin but world opinion and the threat of U.S. boycott forced Germany to include two Jewish athletes in the competition, while one of Germany's most outstanding athletes, Gretel Bergmann, was excluded because of her Jewish ancestry. Jews had been barred from legal or medical professions since 1930; now they were barred, en masse, from civil service and teaching positions. In addition, while Jews were still allowed to own businesses, they were only allowed to do business with fellow Jews. Aryan Germans were prohibited from buying from or selling to Jews.

Sometime in 1936, the Wehrmacht (army) held maneuvers in our area somewhere around Sterbfritz. The cavalry battalion was billeted in Sterbfritz and all vacant stables, ours among them, were requisitioned for their horses. Along with our stables, two officers commandeered one of our vacant bedrooms on the third floor. While they knew we were Jewish and they didn't have to treat us with respect, uncharacteristically, they did so anyway, for which we were grateful.

Kalmann Schuster had been the richest person in Sterbfritz, but he was forced to sell his factory in Sannerz and his businesses in Sterbfritz to one of his employees, an Aryan, because Germans were no longer allowed to work for Jews. One by one, all Jewish rights were dissolved; every day seemed to bring changes—all of them bad for the Jews.

After the Nüremberg laws were passed, Jews were no longer allowed to have stock certificates or government bonds. My Uncle Julius must have had one or the other because the Gestapo demanded the surrender of these papers. Feeling safe in telling them that he gave the papers to our dead father, he thought they would believe him and forget the entire thing. No chance. They came to our house demanding we turn these papers over to them. We knew nothing about it and could not oblige them, but we weren't believed.

Consequently, five Gestapo agents burst into our home searching and ransacking the place. Fearful that we might flush the papers down the toilet, we were forbidden to go to the bathroom alone. If we had to use the toilet, we were accompanied by a Gestapo soldier who waited outside the door. Males were instructed to do their business with the door partly open. Once finished, they inspected the toilet bowel for the papers.

Moving a picture on the living room wall, they discovered my father's wall safe. Herding everyone into the living room, they demanded that Mother open the safe, which she did. They were furious when they found it was empty. Finally, after seven grueling hours, they stormed out of the house, leaving the door open and threatening us with prison if they later found we were lying.

Things went from bad to worse. Shortly after our father's death, our store tenant, Kirst, demanded that we move out of the first-floor apartment. We had no choice but to do so since the law supported his demands. So, we boxed up our belongings and moved to the top floor. Kirst and his family just as quickly pulled up in front of our house with trucks loaded with their furniture and household goods. They now lived in the entire first floor of the house my father built. Feeling that he had the upper hand, Kirst's hostility toward us ballooned into utter contempt. I feared he would hurt me, or worse he would do something to my mother or sisters.

In August of 1936, our Uncle Moritz Steinfeld and his son Günter came to visit to see how we were getting along. Uncle Moritz had many friends in Sterbfritz, so when word got out that he was there many people came to see him. But in order to go upstairs to our section of the house, they had to pass Kirst's apartment, who was by this time openly hostile. Irritated that so many people were coming and going, he posted a sign at the door that said, *"Der Privateingang für Juden ist strengstens verboten."* (This private entrance is strictly prohibited to Jews.)

Now, no one dared to go up the stairs to visit. I remember that at first we weren't upset about it. In fact, we thought it was comical. As the Aryan chokehold increased, our way of dealing with fear was through humor and this incident was no exception. Our mother, sassy and not intimidated by Kirst or his sign, sneaked downstairs one night and changed one letter in the word "Juden." She changed the "u" to an "e." The sign now read, *"Der Privateingang für Jeden ist strengstens verboten."* (The private entrance for everyone is strictly prohibited.)

The next morning while I was at school, Kirst saw the altered sign and he stormed into our apartment demanding to know who had the audacity to change his sign. One by one, my mother's and sisters' the answer was that they knew nothing about it.

Not satisfied, Kirst went to my school to seek me out. Convinced I knew who the culprit was and that I would break down and tell him, he knocked at Lehrer Weidling's classroom door. As Weidling opened the door, I could see Kirst and the Bürgermeister standing in the corridor, and I knew immediately what was to come. As soon as Weidling joined them, I was called into the hallway.

"Did your Uncle Moritz Steinfeld change my sign?" Kirst bellowed loud enough for my classmates to hear through the closed door.

"What sign?" I asked with as much innocence as I could muster. I knew what he was talking about because Mother told us what she had done. I tried with all my might to look as if I didn't know anything. Then Müller took over the questioning. In a flat monotone he recited all the names of the members of my family asking if each, in turn, had altered the sign.

"What sign?" I kept repeating. "I really don't know what you're asking me," I lied. Weidling now opened the door so that the entire classroom could see me, perhaps hoping one of my classmates knew something and would speak up. Or, maybe he thought the public torment he was inflicting would humiliate me into a confession. I don't know what his reason, but after 10 minutes of cruel questioning and when no one said anything, Müller was angered almost beyond self-control. He grabbed my arm, twisting it cruelly, and dragged me toward the outside door.

"I'm going to lock you up until you tell me," he screamed, pulling me viciously out into the street toward the jail in the town hall. Weidling, always up for anti-Jewish drama, dismissed the class and told the students to follow Müller and me. Gleefully joining in on the torment, my classmates taunted me, swearing at me and verbally hurling anti-Jewish slogans at me. At the town hall, Müller continued his savage questioning in his closed-door office, but to no avail. I was more frightened than I had ever been. I was afraid of what they might do to my mother if I told on her. I just couldn't tell them.

Sensing that though I was young I might be tougher than I looked, Müller shoved me into a small room where I fell to my knees on the cold floor. Then he slammed and locked the door and screamed that he would keep me there until I talked—or died. I was frozen with fear. Hours seemed to go by, and I was not given food or water. I don't remember how long I was there, but it seemed like forever, and I was hungry and thirsty.

When my visiting uncle came, I was finally released, and I fell into his arms and sobbed. I was so frightened I was sick to my stomach, and for the rest of the day and part of that night I threw up. Once more safe in my mother's arms, I finally calmed down and was able to sleep. Later I found out that, once again, my sweet classmate, Sofi Hecht, had run to my house to tell my mother what had happened, and it was Uncle Moritz who bravely went to talk to the Bürgermeister. I think it was he who persuaded them that I was just a little boy and knew nothing. That, and my Academy Award acting.

The next morning, I begged my mother not to make me go to school.

"I'm afraid. Don't make me go," I pleaded, tears filling my eyes and spilling down my cheeks. "Please don't make me go," I begged. Afraid for me as well, she agreed I could stay home that day, so I stayed with her as she did her morning chores.

About midmorning, Sofi again knocked on the door. She had been recruited by Lehrer Weidling to hand carry a note to my mother. In the note, he demanded that I come to school at once. The tone of the note, added to the life-threatening pool and tree-tying incidents, made mother and Uncle Moritz realize that my life really was in danger should I stay in Sterbfritz. On the spot, they made the decision to take me away to a safe location. Uncle Moritz packed his bags and told me to do the same. Within the hour, my clothes, a comb and toothbrush were hurriedly stuffed into a suitcase and loaded into the Uncle Moritz' little Adler car. As we headed out of Sterbfritz to his house in Mülhausen, little did I realize that the world I knew had ended.

CHAPTER

SIX

The trip was long. Mülhausen in Thuringen is approximately 150 miles from Sterbfritz and it was 3 p.m. when Uncle Moritz and I arrived. My uncle asked me to stay outside the apartment while he went inside to tell Aunt Erna that I would be staying with them. With the door to the apartment ajar, I could hear shouting.

"What, another Jew?" Aunt Erna screamed. "As if I don't have enough living with three already!"

I was horrified and embarrassed. I wanted to disappear into the seat covers. As young as I was, I knew I wasn't wanted, and wished I were back in Sterbfritz with my mother and sisters. But Uncle Moritz must have been able to mollify his wife because I was permitted to stay, if grudgingly. He took me into the kitchen where I was given bread and cheese. I was really hungry since we had not eaten all day, and I remember how good it tasted. They let me eat as much as I wanted.

The following week I was enrolled in the Mülhausen Jewish parochial school, a school that remained open because the Jewish community there had enough money to support it without government subsidies. Because the last two school years I suffered taunting cruelty from teachers and classmates, I dreaded even the thought of going to the school, and when I did go, I couldn't concentrate because I feared that sooner or later the hate would start all over again. I fell behind in my studies, and because I did so poorly I was not properly prepared to enter the fifth grade. As a consequence, I was kept back in the fourth grade where I slowly began to relax. I soon came to realize that the attacks were not going to happen here and without anti-Semitic stress I was able to excel.

But I wasn't happy. Aunt Erna couldn't, or wouldn't hide her dislike for me, and she made it known I wasn't wanted whenever she got the chance. It was obvious she wished I was gone. Unhappy as I was, I tried to make her like me, but her obvious contempt made me join her in her wish that I wasn't there as well.

Looking to find fault, Aunt Erna invented things I had done wrong so she could reprimand me and point out that I was not as good as her own children. So, it was no surprise that I would get into big trouble if I really did do something wrong—which I did one Saturday after synagogue services.

Passing a fruit stand, I looked longingly at the beautifully arranged fruit. Peaches, plums, grapes, apples and oranges—so beautiful in their colors and fragrance. I wanted a plum in the worst way but had no money; desire overcame good sense, and I took one and quickly hid it in my pocket. I didn't think anyone had seen me, but I was wrong. As luck would have it, the fruit merchant saw me stuff the plum in my pocket, and unfortunately for me, he knew who I was and knew my aunt. That evening, he went to my house and told her what I had done. All hell broke loose, and Aunt Erna went on a tirade. She called me foul names and screamed that I would have to leave. This time, Uncle Moritz could not mollify her and after just six weeks, Uncle Moritz and Aunt Erna threw me out.

Because it still wasn't safe for me to go back to Sterbfritz, another home had to be found and that meant searching out yet another relative who had the room, not to mention the inclination, to take me in. That relative turned out to be another aunt, Tante (Aunt) Rita, who lived in a town called Burghaun. So, for the next four months, Tante Rita Braunschweiger opened her home—and her heart—to me, and I lived happily with her and her sons, Milian, Norbert and Manfred. An older son, Theo, no longer lived at home, which made a room available for me. Tante Rita's gentleness made me feel loved and welcome for the next four months that I would be a guest in her home.

Old enough to work for my room and board, I was given small tasks to do daily along with the most important task of milking the goat twice a day, a job I didn't mind doing because the goat was friendly and I loved goat's milk. But the goat is vivid in my memory for more than the milk she gave. Like many farm kids, it was Aunt Rita's goat that taught me the facts of life.

When Aunt Rita decided to breed her, she made arrangements with a local farmer who had two fine Billy goats. At the time, her three boys were on the road with their jobs, so the task of taking the goat to the breeding barn became mine. Aunt Rita probably thought I would simply deliver the goat and come home right away; the goat staying overnight with the handsome Billy. But the farmer had other ideas. Deciding there was no time like the present, he instructed me to hold our goat's leash while he opened the pen that held one of the males. Romance ensued. I don't know who was more eager, our lovely little she-goat or the devastatingly handsome Billy. At any rate, the deed was done, and slightly red faced, I escorted our brazen hussy back to our barn. This was quite an experience for me at age 10. The world looked entirely different from then on.

Burghaun was a larger town than Sterbfritz and had a Jewish day school in a one-room schoolhouse for grades one through eight. I had excelled in the fourth grade studies I was assigned, so much so that happily I was welcomed back to the fifth grade. For the first time in a long time, I felt good about myself. I had blamed myself for everything that had happened to me. In my heart I knew it was all my fault. If I had been a better behaved, smarter, maybe even a better-looking boy, none of this would have happened. But now things were turning around and going well. I enjoyed going to school, and I made many new friends including one special girlfriend, a pretty girl whom I had no trouble persuading to hide with me in the hayloft and play doctor.

Living with Aunt Rita, I remember being happier than I had been in a very long time. I was free from anti-Semitic torments, I made friends at school, and I found I could master the schoolwork with no problem. I was dearly loved by my Aunt Rita and my cousins, and I loved them back with all my heart.

While I thought of my mother and sisters often, I was not afraid for them since I had only witnessed cruelty to Jewish males. Women, though given the cold shoulder or worse, threatened, called names and denied privileges, had not yet been physically harmed. It was my understanding that they were safe, waiting for the bad times to pass when I would be welcomed home.

The three Braunschweiger cousins still living at home were like older brothers though they were quite a bit older. Norbert and Milian were employed as wine distributors, and they traveled extensively calling on their Jewish customers in central Germany. Norbert had a beautiful, red motor scooter that he used as his mode of transportation, whereas Milian took the train because he traveled to more distant towns. Manfred, a student at the university in Fulda, commuted to class there every day by train.

Fulda, in those days, was a city of about 30,000 people with a fairly large Jewish community and lots of Jewish businesses and retail stores. Fulda was a place where you could buy almost anything.

It was a Jewish shoppers' paradise and only about 10 minutes from Burghaun by the local train that went back and forth every hour.

Norbert had saved all his money to buy his motorbike and was reluctant to let anyone borrow it, especially his brothers. But Manfred needed to go to Fulda one day and wheedled permission from Norbert to let him take it. For some reason, Manfred invited me to go with him so off we went in a blue cloud of exhaust, he in front, and I hanging on for dear life to the luggage rack. Just as we arrived in Fulda it started to rain, a rain that made the streets slick with oil that rose from the asphalt surface. Rounding a curve far too fast for the road conditions, the bike lost traction and skidded onto the shoulder and into the gravel where with increased momentum, the skid spilled us both into the brambles.

Unhurt and laughing uncontrollably, we checked the bike for damage. Finding that no harm had come to the bike, Manfred swore me to secrecy.

"Not one word to Norbert, you hear?" Manfred warned. Knowing that an idle threat would do no good, he decided to buy my silence with a large dish of ice cream at a Jewish-owned confectionery. I agreed not to tell a soul, my lips zipped by ice cream, and I found that my continued silence bought several more ice creams over the next few months.

The absent son, the handsome and suave Theo, lived in northern Germany and had gotten a good job there in a large Jewish department store. Once, when he drove home to visit his mother and brothers, he and Aunt Rita thought it would be good if the three of us drove to Sterbfritz to visit my mother. It was a nice idea, but one that brought more pain than happiness.

We arrived at night so no one would see me, and they had to sneak me into the building. I hadn't seen my mother for more than six months. In her room, she waited anxiously for me to arrive. It was so wonderful to run to her open arms after having been apart for so long. I was so happy to see her I wouldn't leave her side for the two hours we were together. When I finally had to leave, I had to be dragged to the car, and for the next several days I was so homesick I cried almost continuously. I remember I couldn't eat or sleep but Aunt Rita, so loving and gentle, finally calmed me down and life returned to normal.

But my contentment with living with Aunt Rita would soon come to an end, and I was to be taken from her home. Whether she could no longer afford to keep me or if there were other reasons for my going to live in the orphanage in Frankfurt, I'll never know. So many things were happening around me that affected my life, and I was never to know what they were. I only knew that, once again, I was torn from warm and loving people.

Life continued to be bad for the Jews in Germany, and it was determined that I should be placed in the *Waisenhaus* (orphanage) in Frankfurt as soon as I could be accepted. I remember being on a waiting list because the number of children and youths the orphanage could care for was limited. In order to accept a new child another had to leave. When I arrived, I was one of 60 boys and 30 girls.

Orphanages, then as now, take children who are orphans as well as children whose parents are living but unable to care for them financially or otherwise. My sisters had taken jobs as nannies and were not permitted to keep me with them. Bertel graduated from Wolfratshausen and worked for the teacher and cantor in Würzburg, where she was hired to take care of their Down syndrome daughter. Margot was employed as a nanny of two children of a Jewish dentist in Offenbach, and Mother took a position as a live-in companion for an elderly woman. Again, it was no place for a child.

Luckily, or maybe it was planned that way, we were all in the same area, and I could take the streetcar from the orphanage every Sunday to spend the day with my mother. More good luck! My sister Bertel took a job as a nanny with the director of the Jewish *Altersheim* (old age home) on Röderbergweg and the *Waisenhaus*, where I lived, and the Altersheim, where Bertel lived, were right next to each other. It was almost as if we were living under the same roof. At least now we could get together almost every Sunday.

While it was nearly heaven for me to be near my family, life at the orphanage meant yet another adjustment. By the age of 10, this was the fourth home I had had—and three of those homes were without my family. At the orphanage, I was placed in a section with other boys my age and attended school at the Hirsch Realschule. At first, I had difficulty keeping up with the secular and religious studies. Being small in stature and new, I was again a prime target for ridicule. Several boys from larger cities picked on me and teased me about being a country bumpkin. I guess I was.

Abba Goldfinger, a bully and a tough guy, constantly challenged me to wrestling matches. For a long time I refused to take the bait because everyone said he couldn't be beaten, and I was afraid to lose. But one day, right in the middle of the dormitory with the rest of our roommates watching, he started pushing me around egging me into a fight. At first I was timid, refusing to be drawn in. But he wouldn't quit, and by now I had had it and I went into a rage. I was so mad I charged him, got him in a headlock and squeezed as hard as I could. Screaming uncle he surrendered unconditionally, and from that time on I was one of the boys. Nobody bothered me, and I was no longer called the country bumpkin from Sterbfritz.

They say time heals all wounds and as time went by I became acclimated to life at the Waisenhaus. I studied hard and my grades got considerably better. I also caught up in religious classes. I had adjusted to life at the home, and I was again happy.

One of the most significant adjustments I had to make was living in a more strictly Orthodox environment than I had ever experienced. Though I lived a somewhat Orthodox Jewish life in

Sterbfritz, Muhlhausen and Burghaun, the Waisenhaus was even more strict. At all times, boys wore *kippot* (yarmulkes). At home in Sterbfritz, we wore a kippa only during religious school, when we entered the synagogue and when we ate. Because Orthodox observance forbids hair combing on the Sabbath, we wore hairnets under our kippot so that we wouldn't mess up our hair. Also on the Sabbath, so that we wouldn't violate the commandment not to work, which included lifting anything, handkerchiefs were pinned into our pockets to be part of our garments rather than carrying them. It was strict to the nth degree.

At the Waisenhaus, on Friday evening prior to our Sabbath meal, we lined up to receive a blessing from our beloved director, Isador Marks. Friday nights and Saturdays were always festive in the dining room, and I especially liked that the girls from the lower floor joined us for dinner. After the *benshen,* a Yiddish word for the blessing prayer after each meal, we sang Hebrew songs, and one of the boys who was preparing for his bar mitzvah would lead in singing the prayer. At other times, the rest of the boys were asked to lead in prayers, and at first I was reluctant to be the leader. I wasn't sure of my ability, but as time went on I became more proficient in the prayers and even looked forward to being the leader.

After the singing, Uncle Isador told a story or two, and Mrs. Marks, Tante Rosa to us, looked on. A kind and loving person, we loved Rosa Marks as much as we loved Isador. She was our surrogate mother, our mom away from home for those of us who had a living mother, and a real live mom for those whose mothers were deceased. It was special just to be with her because she always treated us like grownups—never talking down to us like so many adults do with children. I remember sitting with her on many an afternoon, helping her darn socks, a skill she taught me and a skill that came in handy later in life when I was a bachelor with holes in my socks. I don't think Tante Rosa ever uttered a cross word, at least not to me. She was my favorite person at the orphanage, and I like to think I was one of her favorites, too.

Tante Marta, Tante Rosa's sister, was the orphanage *Krankenschwester* (nurse). When boys took sick, they were moved to a room called the sick bay where she took care of them. Once, I was extremely sick and ran a dangerously high fever. Tanta Rosa wouldn't let her sister take care of me in the sick bay like the other boys, and she insisted I be moved to the Marks' private quarters where Tanta Rosa cared for me personally. Sick as I was, I knew I was being singled out for special treatment. I had status and I loved it.

At the orphanage, medical care was the best though most illnesses were minor. But on occasion, some of the boys came down with more serious illnesses, and if it was determined to be contagious we were placed into quarantine at the Rothschild Hospital, conveniently located in the next block up from the Waisenhaus. If one of our classmates landed in the quarantine section of the hospital, which faced the street that separated the Waisenhaus from the hospital, those of us on the outside kept him company by waving to the quarantined classmate who waved back if he could. It could be lonely in quarantine.

I landed in the hospital—not the quarantine part but the surgical part—when I came down with a bad case of tonsillitis, and it was determined I needed a tonsillectomy. Helmut Michelson, who was a year older than me, came down with the same malady at the same time, and we wound up in the hospital together sharing a hospital room and going under the knife on the same day. After the surgery, we were kept in the hospital for observance for three or four days, merrily eating all the ice cream we could get, a privilege we would not enjoy once back at the Waisenhaus.

While Helmut was in the hospital with me, he was so sick his real personality didn't surface, but when he felt better and after we returned to the Waisenhaus, his mean disposition surfaced. Because we had spent several days together in the hospital, I felt he was now my good friend, and I smiled at him when he walked over to me at the first meal back at the dining room.

"Open your mouth. I want to see your throat," he said flatly. Complying, I opened my mouth and let him look in. When my mouth was open wide enough for his satisfaction, he threw in a handful of salt. The burning was excruciating, and I lashed out and hit him with my fists. Older and bigger than me, my punches weren't having much of an affect but my friends intervened and stopped the fight before the councilors reprimanded us both. Everyone sympathized with me. But the rules were different here. At the Waisenhaus, it didn't matter who started it. If there was an altercation, both parties got it.

Mr. Siegfried Baumann and Mr. Seligman were the two male counselors who would have intervened in the fight between Helmut and me if it had escalated to that. Fortunately, it didn't. When Baumann and Seligman weren't counseling, they were also the Hebrew teachers, and fortunately for me I later found out, I had a personal connection with Siegfried Baumann.

Baumann knew his former classmate and best friend, Georg Friess, lived in Sterbfritz, and when he found out that I was from Sterbfritz, he nearly jumped with joy. When I told him Friess had been my Hebrew teacher, he all but throttled me for more information. Baumann hadn't heard from Friess since they left school, and he quizzed me intensely about what he was doing and how he was. He told me how great a soccer player and all-around athlete Friess was at the seminary, and I told him all I knew about Lehrer Friess and his motorcycle. Tactfully, I left out the part about his affair with his landlady, Elsie Hecht. Even at such a young age, I possessed good judgment and good sense.

I liked living at the home. The dormitories were divided according to age and in my room, nine boys, the ages ranged from 10 to 12, were bunked. I had lots of friends, but my two best friends were Fritz Strauss and Hermann (Dudu) Bacherach.

Friday afternoon was bath time. Though it seems archaic in America today, where many new houses have private bathrooms for each bedroom, in German homes we were lucky to have a bathroom on our floor. Our bathroom was the deluxe version with three bathtubs. On weeknights, we would line up in front of the many sinks to thoroughly wash ourselves. A towel and washcloth were issued that was to be used the entire week.

For bathing, the rule was that two boys shared a tub, with the restriction for modesty's sake and for reasons I later became aware of, that we were required to wear bathing trunks while in the tub. I remember Dudu and I taking our bath and how he confided in me that he was disturbed that he had only one testicle. Some time later, he told me he felt better about the whole thing after he was able to have an erection.

As young boys with only the male teachers in our circle of acquaintances to serve as role models, we boys felt important when an older boy from another dormitory paid attention to us. One night, an older boy came into our room and climbed into my bed with me. At first, I was flattered that he chose me, but the feeling turned to disgust when I found out he wanted me to play with his penis. Not only that, he wanted to do the same to me. I didn't know what this was all about, but I was filled with revulsion and knew it was wrong. Jumping out of bed, I screamed at him and told him to leave.

He stalked out of the room and still trembling, I hopped back into bed. The commotion woke my dormitory buddy in the next bed. When I told him what had happened, he told me to calm down, that it wasn't the end of the world, and the guy had tried to do the same to him the day before—with the same result. Shaken, this was my first encounter with homosexuality, but it wasn't until many years later that I was able to put a label on the behavior.

Other than that incident, days at the Waisenhaus were pretty conventional with a routine that was comforting. We were awakened at 6:30 a.m. and were expected to wash, brush our teeth and attended morning religious services at our in-house synagogue. Then, off to the dining room for breakfast where we sat at assigned seats at long tables.

Counselor Baumann sat at the end of my table, and I was proud that my seat was next to his on the right—an honored location. After the meal, one boy was selected to lead the after-the-meal prayer, though everybody knew the prayer by heart. The routine was a comfort. The prayers were a comfort, too. I was content.

We were isolated from the outside world, almost cloistered, but upon occasion, worldly influences crept in. Somehow, I got hold of a dime novel. I didn't read it, but the cover looked pretty racy. I had the book tucked under my shirt and proudly showed it off to my classmates during recess. One of the teachers who knew my sister saw the book and confiscated it, threatening to tell my sister of my misdeed. I always wondered if he read it before he threw it away— if, indeed, he threw it away.

Once a week we had mandatory singing classes taught by Lehrer Neumann, a man so namby-pamby we nicknamed him Neukäs, the name of a kind of soft, German cheese. In the class, in addition to singing in a chorus, each of us was required to sing a solo. I was petrified. All I could think of was Weidling forcing me to sing anti-Semitic songs while the whole class jeered and made fun of me for being Jewish. But Neumann insisted, and I started to cry. Sympathetic, he relented, and that was the last time he tried to make me sing.

At 12:30, school was let out and we Waisenhaus boys walked together back to the home. But, anti-Semitism found us here, too, and we had to walk in groups to protect each other from attacks by the Hitler Jugend. After lunch, we had free time until 3 p.m. when we attended Hebrew classes. We also studied Chumash (the Bible) Kitzer Schulchan Aurach (laws) and Gemmora (Talmud). After a full hour of studies, it was back to the dining room for hot chocolate and bread with jelly. Before complete darkness set in, we returned to the synagogue for afternoon and evening prayers.

Life was usually routine at the home, but routine is what we needed. The upheavals some of us experienced made routine a welcome condition. Routine was something we could count on, and it balanced the unknown, scary world outside our doors.

Our routine went like this: Every night for an hour and a half before dinner we did compulsory homework for the Realschule. Dinner was always served at 8 p.m., and then we got an hour of free time. During free time, we could play board games like chess and checkers. Marbles were always fun, and the favorite make-believe game was a German version of cowboys and Indians. My best friend, Fred Strauss, always instigated this game and always took the best role for himself. We called the game *Flatfüss* (Flatfeet) referring to the Indians.

Part of this game's fun was to explore the unknown parts of the building like the home's sub-basement where the heating plant and other utilities were housed. From the basement we'd sneak up to the attic where the removable roof was used in the autumn festival of Succoth. We weren't supposed to be there, but we were brave and explored all the old building's nooks and crannies.

Saturday was a special day—from sundown on Friday to sundown on Saturday was the Sabbath. After getting dressed in our best attire, we'd go to the synagogue to attend *Shachris* services as well as the reading of the weekly portion from the Safer Torah (scriptures). This service would last at least an hour and a half to two hours, after which a light breakfast was served around 10 a.m. At about 11 a.m., we all reassembled in the synagogue for the Musaf service, and after Musaf we were served the main meal of the day. After a rest period, we had religious studies until 4 p.m. The afternoon service and the reading of the Torah was a rather brief service, and after dark we returned to the synagogue for the evening service. *Havdalah*, the ceremony to conclude the Sabbath, was conducted in the dining room prior to our evening meal. It was the same every Sabbath—something we could count on in a world where there was nothing much else we could count on.

I loved the Jewish holidays; they were always special to me as they still are today. On *Pesach* (Passover), we celebrated with a seder for two nights (Israel is the only place in the world where Pesach is celebrated only one night), and for this holiday the girls could join us. Uncle Isador conducted the service, which lasted way into the night. Joyfully, we sang the prayers and Uncle Isador told many stories. The food, too, was special on Pesach.

On Succoth, or Sukkot, we had all our meals in the attic under the removable roof. The word *sukkot* (the singular is *sukkah*) means "booths," and the removable roof symbolized the temporary dwellings, or sukkot, the Jews resided in during the 40 years they wandered in the desert. Today, observant Jews construct symbolic wall-less booths in their backyards and decorate them with fruit and vegetables. These sukkot represent these very same booths. All meals are joyfully taken in the booths during the holiday that lasts seven days.

On Chanukah, which is a minor holiday that has, in self defense, grown to a size all out of proportion in countries where Christmas is celebrated, we received walnuts and *dreidels* to play the traditional dreidel game (a sort of gambling game). I was always good at playing the dreidel and often won everybody's walnuts, which I happily gave back after I won a pile of them that were too big to carry.

Sunday afternoons were free days, and we were allowed to leave the home and do whatever we wanted. If we had money, we occasionally went to a movie. My sister Bertel was now working at the Altersheim next door and making good money. When she had extra, she would give me 20 marks for Fred and me to go to a movie, a wonderful experience that opened our eyes to so much more in the world. Even if it was fiction and the result of Hollywood glitz, we loved it! That day, we saw "Billy the Kid" with Robert Taylor, complete with good guys, bad guys (who always got it in the end) six shooters and horses. I remember I was supposed to bring back the change to Bertel, but somehow I lost the money. She worked hard for that money and was always thinking about ways she could spend it to make me happy. That I lost it makes me sad to this day.

In the summer of 1938, a boxing rematch between Max Schmeling and Joe Louis was fought in the United States. The time difference between New York and Europe was six hours, so the fight was broadcast in Germany around 2 a.m. One of our roommates had a crystal radio set, and we all wanted to listen. But in order to be awake at broadcast time, we decided we would take turns staying awake. The boy whose turn it was to be awake at fight time was to wake all of us when the fight started.

We tuned the radio to the right station but it was hard to hear because the reception was weak; the crystal set could hardly pick up the broadcast. The kids closest to the radio listened and repeated everything the announcer said so we all knew what was happening—we could feel every blow.

Emotions were high. After all, we were Germans, and even though we were persecuted for being Jews, many of us rooted for the German guy. Others rooted for Louis who in their minds represented the underdog, like the Jews, triumphing over the Nazis.

It was incredibly exciting, and we found it hard not to make noise so we wouldn't wake our councilors. By the time the fight was transmitted to us, in New York it had been over a long time, but since we hadn't heard the results it was as if it were being fought right then. When Joe Louis won, I was glad. Maybe the Jews would win, too.

Life was pretty good then. My sister Bertel's boyfriend was leaving for the United States and couldn't take most of his belongings with him, so he bestowed one of his most prized possessions, his bicycle, on me. Only two of the other kids owned bicycles, so I was ever so popular now with everyone asking to ride it. I was a pretty good kid, and I remember I willingly shared the bike with the kids I could count as friends. Taking turns, we all learned to ride it but not without a number of spills that resulted in skinned knees and hands. Skinned knees and the scabs that followed were a way of life back then. I couldn't remember a time when I didn't look at my knees to see scabs in various stages of healing. I think I must have been about 13 when I noticed that my knees were scab free, a condition I felt good about because I realized the smooth condition of my knees was a precursor to adulthood.

While the school was Orthodox and observed all the Jewish religious and dietary laws, the administrators were not as strict in observance as the Chasidic Jews. Until my life in Frankfurt I had never seen a Chasidic Jew, and it seemed very strange to me to be in school with boys who wore long *peyot* (side locks). Also, we wore our *ztiztis* (shirt fringes) tucked into our pants, whereas the Chasidic boys wore their zitztis on the outside, hanging outside their pants almost to knee length.

Several of my Waisenhaus friends and I were invited to a Chasidic classmate's bar mitzvah. Because it was on a Saturday morning and transportation on the Sabbath with any conveyance other than the feet God provided was prohibited, we walked to the storefront synagogue where the bar mitzvah was being held. The synagogue was the first Chasidic synagogue I had experienced, and I felt as strange in that strict environment as would a non-Jew.

Until then, the German synagogues I had attended had services that were so quiet you could hear a pin drop. The only voice one heard belonged to the prayer leader and then only when portions of the prayers were to be read in unison would other voices be heard. Otherwise, everyone said or read the prayers silently. Here, everyone chanted prayers in their own time—definitely not in unison. The din in the room was deafening with the men seemingly trying to gain the reputation for being the most pious by the decibel level of his chanting.

In addition, I was used to seeing men wear prayer shawls worn over their shoulders, similar to a woman's shawl, with the ends allowed to hang at their sides unfettered. Here, I saw for the first time men covering their entire heads with the prayer shawls. It was also the first time I had seen *peyes*, the long side locks worn by Chasidic men. It was as unique an experience to me, a Jew, as it would have been to a non-Jew.

While the bar mitzvah was similar to the ones I had witnessed, here the boy read the entire Torah portion, not just a section of it as we did. It took a long time to read the whole thing, but he did well. All Chasidic boys were, and are, well schooled in Hebrew and reading the Torah.

In America today, a bar mitzvah is cause for celebration with a huge themed party following the synagogue services. At this bar mitzvah, the only celebration was the men dancing in the sanctuary with the bar mitzvah boy allowed to dance while holding the Torah scroll in his arms. The celebration was not a party but simply the honor of becoming a man and joining other Jewish men in a tradition that is 2,000 years old.

CHAPTER
SEVEN

In October 1938, all German-Jewish citizens of Polish ancestry were rounded up and forced to go back to Poland. Their businesses, homes, farms and factories were confiscated by the German government, and they left with nothing. In Paris, a German national named Grinzpan became so enraged by this act he entered the German embassy and demanded to speak with the German ambassador. When he was told the ambassador was not there, he shot and killed the ambassador's aide. The Nazi government declared that this heinous act was the result of a Jewish conspiracy to eliminate the German people.

Consequently, on November 9, 1938, Kristallnacht (the Night of Broken Glass), a horrendously evil act against German Jews, took place all over Germany. During the night, Jewish stores were broken into, display windows smashed, and store interiors looted and demolished. Many Jews were dragged from their homes into the streets and mercilessly beaten. ...Many were killed as their children looked on in helpless horror. Synagogues were torched, ancient Torah scrolls desecrated and burned, and in the aftermath entire sections of cities and towns that were inhabited by Jews lay in ruins.

"In November of 1938 I was awakened one morning when it was still dark by a friend who pounded the window of my bedroom. "The synagogue is on fire,"

he shouted, and "you must not miss this spectacle." The synagogue was right in front of our house on a hill, and I could see everything. We didn't think of the people or their horror, we only felt excitement. That day, the Jews were taken out of their houses and assembled on a huge soccer field where they were crammed onto trucks and carried away to face unspeakable terrors. We were told that they were taken to work camps."

"We did not see the writing on the wall and maybe we did not want to."— "Defeating the Totalitarian Lie, a Former Hitler Youth Warns America" *by Hilmar Von Campe*

Life changed drastically in November of 1938. The infamous Kristallnacht was perpetrated against German Jewry on the night of November 9. Our counselors alerted us as to what happened in the city, and we could see smoke at a distance from the burning synagogues. As children, we didn't get the full import of the situation (perhaps that was a good thing), and we felt safe as far as our lives were concerned. We had full confidence in our adult leaders and believed them when they assured us that no harm would come to us.

On November 10, the counselors assembled us, including the girls, in the dining room for some reason I don't remember. What I do remember is that while we were in the meeting, several Jewish men from the neighborhood pounded on the orphanage door begging to hide there from the Gestapo. The Nazis were rounding up all males over the age of 16 to arrest them, and they hoped the sanctuary wouldn't be searched.

Fearing that their presence would upset us, Uncle Isador asked them not to come into the dining room but to go to the orphanage's synagogue and make believe they were attending a service. He didn't turn them away, but he didn't want us to be frightened either.

Why I remember this, I'll never know, but for lunch that day we were served red cabbage and boiled potatoes. Maybe it's so indelibly printed on my memory because during the meal several Brown Shirt Nazis stormed into the dining hall looking for the two Jews who were hiding in the synagogue. Searching everywhere, they finally found them in the synagogue and dragged them by the hair to the outside of the building where they beat them bloody. Then, leaving them in the street to die, they took the Safer Torahs from the Ark, tore them to shreds and crushed them into the floor with their boots.

From the dining room, we could hear the men screaming and the sound of the Torahs being ripped to pieces. Then, suddenly, there was silence. Frozen with fear, some of the boys began to whimper quietly but stopped when the Gestapo once again burst through the dining room door, swinging clubs at anyone in their path. Herding the councilors to the far side of the room and away from the children, they arrested all the male teachers, councilors and older boys and forced them into the back of closed trucks to be taken who knew where. It was pandemonium with everyone crying and screaming.

Isador Marks was spared because during the commotion he slid unnoticed under a table. Children standing nearby pulled the tablecloth lower to the floor concealing him as he huddled there. After the Gestapo left, he emerged and restored order as best he could. It took almost an hour to settle the children down.

A few days later, the male teachers and older boys who were taken by the Gestapo were set free, but the stories they told were incomprehensible. One boy had his hands tied behind his back and was interrogated about the location of other Jews who might be hiding from the Nazis. When he wouldn't answer, they beat him mercilessly. Saying to himself, "I can take this" as he was being beaten, he was able to endure the punishment without breaking. None of the captives were allowed to go to the bathroom and were made to sit on the floor in their own excrement. It was many years, half a lifetime to be more exact, before I could eat or even look at red cabbage without thinking of that horrible day.

Bertel somehow got word to me that she and Margot were okay and no harm had come to them during Kristallnacht. Mother, who had returned to Sterbfritz when her job was terminated because of the death of the woman she had been caring for, had survived the onslaught as well. She told me that the Sterbfritz Jews had been forewarned that something terrible was going to happen to all German Jews on November 9, and Mother managed to leave Sterbfritz on November 8, going to Brückenau to hide at Tante Gustel's house. Finding that Brückenau was not safe for Jews either, she managed to get to Frankfurt to stay with Bertel at the Altersheim.

Shortly after Mother's arrival, Margot also managed to get from Offenbach to the home. My sisters and mother were all together at last, and I was nearby. The danger seemed to have passed, and we once again looked forward to the future. It was easy to think the worst was over because it was impossible to comprehend that it could be worse than it already was. We lived in the moment.

Mother soon got a new job as a laundress. But her employers, the Liebermanns, recognized mother's skills and recommended to their board that she take over their position as director when they immigrated to Peru as they planned to do. So, a few days after Kristallnacht, Mother became the new director of the Altersheim, a job she handled with skill and efficiency. Life was good again, and we tried not to think about the past and concentrate on the present and the future.

During this time, many Jewish schools were closed, some with windows and doors boarded shut, and others left open but expropriated for other uses by the government. I never knew if the Hirsch Realschule was closed, but we were no longer allowed to go there and then attended classes at the home. Early in December, the influx of children increased immensely. My first cousin, Herbert Steinfeld, was admitted, and he and I shared my bed because there weren't enough beds to go around.

I loved having my mother and my sisters so close to me again. Only a wooden fence separated the Waisenhaus and the Altersheim, and we were able to loosen two vertical fence boards in such a way that I could swing the boards open (Tom Sawyer style) and sneak into the Altersheim daily to be with my family. Mother would always have something nice for me to eat, and occasionally I would bring a friend along to share some of the goodies as well. Food at the Waisenhaus was no longer plentiful, and many of us were hungry so I was happy Mother could give me more food than I was given at the home.

Three days after Kristallnacht, Uncle Moritz Schuster turned up on the doorstep at Altersheim, now seeking refuge for himself. When I saw him, I barely recognized him because his appearance had changed so much. After he was given a good meal and given the opportunity to rest a bit, he told us his story.

Unlike Mother, Uncle Moritz, my father's brother, was in Sterbfritz on the night of November 9. He refused to believe that a grown man, strong and healthy, was in any real danger, and he failed to take the warnings seriously. But on Kristallnacht, not only were the Brown Shirts killing Jews and destroying their property, ordinary German citizens turned deadly and ran in packs through the streets, killing and maiming any Jews they saw or pulling them from their homes if they hid.

Several hoods from another town stormed into Uncle Moritz' house and dragged him from his kitchen into the street where they beat him to the ground. Seeing her fallen husband through the window, his wife Toni ran to his defense. Hitting them with her fists, she screamed for them to stop, then fell to her knees trying to cover Uncle Moritz' body with her own. But instead of making them stop, her interference infuriated them, and turning their attention now to Toni they beat and kicked her, too, driving her back into the house. With Aunt Toni dispensed with, they resumed punching and kicking Uncle Moritz, leaving him only when they thought he was dead.

Afraid to go out into the street again, Aunt Toni could only watch helplessly from the window. Moritz lay there, battered and bloody until dark when he was able to crawl back to the house. Aunt Toni helped him inside and did what she could to bind his wounds.

Later that week, he and other Sterbfritz men were ordered by the Bürgermeister to report to Hanau where they would be put in prison because the law decreed that all men up to the age of 65 were to be incarcerated. Younger than 65, Uncle Moritz was lucky to look much older, and the official made the erroneous assumption that Uncle Moritz was too old to be incarcerated. Released, he realizing that this kind of luck would come only once, and taking advantage of this fortuitous happenstance he managed to get to the Altersheim to seek refuge.

Afraid that he would be caught and all of us put in prison, Mother, Bertel and Margot hid him in a storage room in the attic and concealed the door by dragging a large wardrobe in front of it. After several days, Uncle Moritz felt he was safe and emerged. Aunt Toni then joined him, and they moved to the safety of an apartment that had been occupied by a family that had visas to leave Germany. Even now, only the men were attacked and put in prison; the women were left unharmed.

Early in 1939, the world began to understand how bad the situation was for Jews in Germany, and several European countries tried to save Jewish children by admitting German- and Austrian-Jewish children refugees. Eleven children from Frankfurt were randomly picked to go to France, and I was one of them. I don't know the criteria used to choose these 11 children, but we were told that time was of the essence and to quickly pack our scant belongings. We left Frankfurt in March of 1939. Our adult escort was Frau Marks, the sister-in-law of Isador Marks. While we were chosen to go to France, others went to England, Belgium, Holland and Switzerland. Before leaving Frankfurt for France, we learned that a transport of 35 children would leave the Waisenhaus for Palestine with Uncle Isador Marks as the adult escort. My cousin Herbert Steinfeld was among that group.

Split up again, it was heartbreaking to leave my mother and sisters. I can imagine how my mother's heart broke not knowing for sure but suspecting that she would never see her only son again. She felt much more fear for my safety than for her own, and as she kissed me goodbye, she told me she would always love me, and that I should be brave. At the age of 12, I left Germany for good. My childhood was over.

CHAPTER
EIGHT

In the postwar France of 1939, the economy was strong and the outlook bright. The French government, having just signed a joint declaration of peace with Germany, felt its eastern borders were secure. But soon after, in June of 1940, Germany broke its treaty and invaded. The Maginot Line, that is, fortifications along the French border, failed, allowing German troops to storm over France, and Parisians literally abandoned Paris in order to seek asylum in Vichy (unoccupied) France. With roads and highways blocked by thousands of cars, bicycles and carts, escape from German troops to French soil unoccupied by German troops was slow and arduous. Escape to a neutral territory was nearly impossible.

At the border between Germany and France, German customs agents entered the train to search our luggage. Pawing through my belongings, they found the only thing of value I had: my silver *kiddush* (wine) cup. This they confiscated along with any valuables they found on any of the other children. They also confiscated our money, allowing us to keep only 10 Deutschmarks each. The uniformed German agents were vicious and intimidating, pushing us if we got in their way and yelling obscenities at us. Frightened to our bones, we timidly cowered in our seats, trying to make ourselves as small as possible until we crossed the border and were able to thankfully plant our feet firmly on French soil.

We weren't allowed to continue our journey on the German train, which then stopped at the border and prepared for a return trip back. Walking, we carried our own bags across the border, bags that were lighter now, but bags that held all the possessions we had in the world.

It was a relief to find that the French officials welcomed us and escorted us to a French train. Once aboard, we settled in. Sleep deprived, many used each other's shoulders or duffle bags as pillows. I remember being so tired I could have slept standing up, but at the same time my face was glued to the window. France was a whole new world, and my eyes drank in the scenery. It was beautiful. There were tall mountains, and wildflowers bloomed everywhere. I had never seen mountains before. My part of Germany was flatter with rolling hills that weren't very high. This land was more beautiful than I could even have imagined. Soon, we went through more populated parts of the country going through towns and small cities en route to Paris. Late in the afternoon of March 8, 1939, we steamed into Paris.

Madame Baroness De Rothschild, herself, was on the station platform and greeted us when we arrived at the Paris train station. It was she who escorted us to the Rothschild Hospital. I thought her the most elegant woman I had ever seen, and she was as kind as she was beautiful. Tall and lanky, she was a sophisticated woman who wore makeup, unusual for women in those days. I remember her bright red lipstick and rouged cheeks. Her beautifully coiffed hair was a medium brown color, and she wore an expensive two-piece suit—a skirt with a matching jacket—and high heeled shoes. In my mind's eye, I can still see her. She looked like a queen, and I was mesmerized by her beauty as well as her kindness.

She spoke to us in German, welcoming us to France. She said she would take us to some fun places, and she hoped we would enjoy ourselves and have a pleasant time. She was gracious, talking to us as if we were adults and never talking down to us. Her manor was so loving, a feeling we were starved for, that we were immediately drawn to her and felt comfortable in her presence. I didn't know her importance then. I didn't know she was a famous and influential woman, but I was later to learn. In retrospect, I can hardly believe this very important lady wanted to spend time with us. But she did, and I have loved her ever since.

At the hospital, we were again warmly welcomed, this time by French nurses. It had been a long trip from the train station, and I vividly remember I had to go to the bathroom in the worst way. I was embarrassed to ask where the bathroom was, but bladder pain overcame my bashfulness and I asked, in German, where it was located. Not knowing German, the nurses didn't understand what I wanted. Frustrated, I resorting to pantomime, jumping up and down and pointing to my crotch. Finally comprehending, one of the nurses rushed me to the restroom. I must have been a sight because they laughed hysterically.

We were one of the first groups of children to arrive at the hospital but later that evening more groups appeared, some from Berlin, others from Stettin. More and more children came to the hospital making the accommodations cramped, but after two or three days, everyone was split up again, and we were taken to various children's homes in and around Paris. My friends, Eric Greene (Erich Gruenebaum) and Fred Strauss (Fritz Strauss) and I were sent to a very Orthodox boy's school, Ecôle Maimonides, in the Bois de Boulogne.

Before leaving Frankfurt, I had prepared for my upcoming bar mitzvah and had studied hard; I knew my Torah portion well. I didn't know that Jewish boys in other countries had bar mitzvoth, and I was afraid that because of leaving Germany I wouldn't be able to become bar mitzvah. As luck would have it, two weeks after I entered school I was taken to a synagogue on Saturday morning to recite my Sidre (Vayikro). While waiting to be called to the bimah, the rabbi spoke in French and at length to the congregation. I never found out what he said, but when it was my turn to recite the Torah portion, I could see many of the women in the balcony were crying. It seemed so sad to me that I broke up and started crying too. Soon, everyone in the sanctuary was crying—me, the rabbi, the cantor, the people in the sanctuary. The cantor was the first to regain composure, and once under control he was able to calm me down and I completed the reading.

Passover is very important in Judaism, and the school was closed for the holiday. All the French boys were sent home to celebrate Passover with their families, and the three of us German kids with no homes to go to, were sent to the Rothschild Hospital. The baroness herself again appeared out of nowhere and had taken charge of the hospital. For a week we lived the life of Riley. Once more, the baroness made sure we were well taken care of and kept entertained. She escorted us to the Paris Zoo, to the Eiffel Tower and on a boat ride on the river Seine. At the zoo, we rode on a camel and an elephant while she watched, waved and occasionally shouted funny things to us. I was in love with her.

My bar mitzvah was very close to Passover. According to the Jewish religion, at the age of 13 boys officially become men. It is the age when a boy is considered to know right from wrong, can act upon that knowledge and take responsibility for his actions. For girls, the age is 12 when she becomes bat mitzvah.

Having undergone the bar mitzvah ritual, I was officially a man, and suddenly I was manfully aware of girls. I was developing into a handsome youth, a fact that did not go unnoticed by the girls. Once, on a six-week outing to an ancient castle in Maubisson in the town of Point Oise, Friedel Chanales joined us with a group from Vienna. Friedel, sophisticated and mature, was the oldest of our group at Maubison, and consequently her physical development was more advanced than the other girls—a fact I didn't fail to observe.

Her father was a prominent rabbi in Vienna, which made me think twice about any advances I might make toward her. But Friedel took control of the situation by inviting me to take a walk in the woods—alone. Once far away from the others, she grabbed me by the shoulders and kissed me firmly on the mouth. I had never kissed a girl before, and the sensation made my head spin and my knees go weak. The baroness was replaced by a 10-year-old girl. I immediately fell deeply and totally in love with the beautiful, well-developed Friedel Chanales.

Unfortunately, Friedel didn't return the feeling and thereafter ignored me. Perhaps my kiss wasn't up to par, or maybe she was using me as a practice dummy for kisses that would later be bestowed upon another boy. I'll never know. But I must have passed some kind of test because later she decided that I should be paired with her best friend Sonya Kislowitz who was also from Vienna. Sonya was pretty, too, and an accomplished pianist for a 13-year-old girl, and I liked her. But it was Friedel whom I loved and with whom I was now infatuated. Friedel made me hold hands with Sonya and repeat after her, *"Hareh at mikadashis L,"* which meant that we were married. While we knew this was only a game, it pained me no end that I couldn't say the words with my beloved Friedel.

But while Friedel had my heart, everyone knew, including me, that Evelyn Fuchs was really the most beautiful girl of all at Maubison. Ever the matchmaker, Friedel paired her up with Fritz Strauss. I don't recall how Fritz felt about all this or even how Evelyn felt. Most everyone was matched up by the fair Friedel, and

I don't know if those who weren't matched were glad or not to have escaped her matchmaking.

In 1938—1939, the Organisation pour la Sante et l'Education, *better known as the OSE, a private Jewish organization, established homes throughout France for refugee children. Most of the children were Jewish, but some were the children of political undesirables. In September 1939, there were four such homes in Montmorency that were filled with children from 3 years of age to 15 years of age. A fourth and fifth home (mostly castles) would soon be purchased by OSE since the already established homes were bursting at the seams and could house no more. Saving children was the OSE's main concern, and they saved as many as they could—possibly more than a thousand.*

The first OSE children's home in France was opened in the Fall of 1938 in Montmorency, a suburb of Paris; this may be considered the mother institution of the great network of children's homes which were later spread by the OSE over the whole of France. ...In February 1939, children started to come directly from Austria and Germany into the new house of the Union OSE at Montmorency. 'May Jewish children go into this garden?' they asked timidly when they entered the park of their new home Villa Helvetia. But soon the garden and the house of the villa belonged to them. Soon the evil dream of the persecutions from which they and their families had suffered in Hitler-Germany was overcome and merry laughter filled all the rooms and the garden up to the high tops of the hundred-year-old trees.—"Fifty Years of OSE" *by Ernest Papanek*

It was now time to leave Maubison and much to our surprise we didn't go back to the home in Paris. Instead, we were bused to a home operated by the OSE at the Villa Helvetia in Montmorency, 15.9 km west of Paris. There, we were reunited with the rest of the Frankfurt group.

The executive director of the home was a kindly man and a socialist named Ernst Papanek from Vienna. Papanek was a world-renowned educator and the education minister of Austria prior to the Anschluss, the political union that unified Nazi Germany and Austria in 1938. Now in 1939, he had agreed to head up one of the homes for refugee children that were run by OSE—the Organisation pour la Sante et l'Education. Papanek's wife, Dr. Helena Papanek, was a psychiatrist. The couple had two sons who also lived at the villa as well as several other adult counselors, all originally from Germany. Dr. Helena, as we called her, was also our physician.

Old run-down, dirty buildings were made up-to-date and hygienic. Speed was necessary, for the hunting down of Jewish children was under way in Germany. …There was no question of teaching them at first. In the beginning, there was simply nothing else to consider save coaxing to life a single smile, awakening a single interest in these stunned boys and girls." —a description of the Jewish children who were taken to safety at Villa Chesnaie by author Otto Zoff in his book, "They Shall Inherit the Earth."

After a short time in Montmorency, the Orthodox home in Eaubonne, a short distance from Montmorency, was opened to accommodate us and all the Orthodox children who were transferred there. The home was in the Villa Chesnaie, a large sprawling house that was rented from a Parisian family. Enormous, the house was large enough to accommodate all 60 children.

The villa had three floors plus a full basement with the main floor consisting of a large room that we used as our recreation and general-use room. Adjoining the main room was a glass-enclosed addition, which was to become our synagogue. On the other side of the main room was our dining room, and adjoining it was the newly remodeled kitchen. The house was cold because it had no central heating system, but OSE contracted with a Paris company to install steam-heat radiators in all the rooms with the heating plant in the cellar. While the work was being done I watched closely, fascinated with what the steamfitters were doing. I was so interested that I volunteered to be their helper, an offer they gladly accepted, and for the next several weeks I got my first lessons in pipefitting, a skill that was to come in handy at various times throughout my life.

Dr. Ernst Papanek was now the executive director of both Montmorency and Eaubonne. Just under him in authority was the first director, a 27-year-old man named Paul Weinberg. Weinberg knew us well since, small world that it is, he had been the Boy Scout leader in Maubison. A favorite with the boys, we were sad when Weinberg's directorship was terminated after only a very short period of time. He was dismissed because he tried to take certain liberties with the older girls. What his transgressions were we were never told, but we missed him all the same.

The next director was Boris Ginodman, a 42-year-old Russian bachelor who had worked or World ORT, a Jewish education and vocational training organization in Cologne. He, too, was a kind man, and we learned to love him as much as Paul. Boris was very talented in many ways. Fluent in Hebrew as well as Russian, he taught us songs in both languages in addition to directing and organizing plays. One of the plays was with a cast of three: a father named Knopp and his two daughters. The idea was that Knopp was looking to find suitable husbands for his daughters, a theme that may have also been the inspiration for Teva the milkman in "Fiddler on the Roof."

Another skit was taken from the opera "Die Fledermaus." One of the boys played the drunken jailer, and another played the baron. In one scene, the jailer was supposed to kick a dog behind the scenes. The yelping dog was none other than me, Heinz Schuster, a role I had the greatest fun playing.

Once, since our plays were looked upon with such favor in the community, under Ginodman's direction we performed "The

Circus" at a local school, which was open to Eaubonne's general public. It was a huge success. I remember how much fun it was to take bows at the play's conclusion. The smell of greasepaint, the roar of the crowd! I can still feel the excitement.

I think being a ham was a trait I was born with. I loved being the center of attention, which wasn't always a good thing. Once, I overslept and was late for Boris Ginodman's before-breakfast calisthenics class. Knowing I had to hurry or I would miss the class, I had no time to dress but ran to the class in my pajamas. Everyone thought it was funny, and that I did it for a laugh. Maybe I did. I loved to make people laugh.

But before long we once more lost a favorite director. There seemed to have been a rift between Ginodman and Ernst Papanek, and Ginodman was relieved of his duties as director of the Eaubonne group. This experience was traumatic for all of us kids. It seemed like we were always losing people we loved, a loss that started with the loss of our families when we had to leave them behind. It seemed like a way of life, and it was something we never got used to. The pain of loss was with us constantly. It still is.

The French ORT organization knew of Boris Ginodman's background and asked him to organize a carpentry training center at Tourelle. This facility was established at the third OSE home under Papanek's charge. Tourelle was established when France accepted many children from the ship the St. Louis. The St. Louis was a German luxury ocean liner whose 900 passengers, made up of Jewish men, women and children, were headed to Cuba for temporary asylum while waiting for permission to enter the United States. All had the necessary documents to leave Germany, purchased dearly with money they somehow scrounged or borrowed since most had their assets confiscated before they were allowed to leave Germany. Upon their arrival at the port of Havana, the passengers were refused entry by the Batista government. The captain, Gustav Schroeder, sympathized with the plight of the German Jews and did his best to persuade authorities to let the disheartened passengers disembark. But Nazi influence in the Cuban government and anti-Jewish rallies organized by Cuban Nazis worked the Cuban island into a near anti-Semitic frenzy. The decision was made that no one could disembark, and it was recommended that the ship return to Germany.

After several days sailing off the coast of the United States with communications with the Roosevelt State Department garnering not even the least encouraging feedback, the ship returned to Europe. It landed in France, but France, Belgium and Holland refused to let any of the adults disembark. Children, however, were allowed to go ashore. These youngsters, known as the Kubaners, ended up at the Tourelle home where our beloved Boris Ginodman had been transferred.

Because ORT leased the Tourelle stables for the newly established carpentry shop, we got to know the Kubaners. Tourelle was a 20-minute walk from Villa Chesnaie, and several of us boys from Eaubonne became cabinetry apprentices along with the Kubaners and happily studied cabinetry under the tutelage of our beloved Boris. Some of the Kubaners came to live with the Eaubonne group as well. The Kubaners became our close friends, and our hearts ached for them. In spite of our own losses, theirs seemed worse. To be so close to freedom and yet so far from it was unfathomable. It seemed like the entire world hated us because we were Jews, and for reasons we simply couldn't grasp.

OSE was highly influenced by the ORT philosophy of teaching children a trade. So, in addition to academic studies, we were to learn a craft. At Eaubonne, a 19-year-old master shoemaker from Hungary taught shoemaking and leatherworks. He was young to have such a mastery of the skill, but his talent provided a source of learning for those boys who had no interest in cabinetmaking, the other job skill taught at the school.

The girls of Eaubonne and Tourelle learned to be dressmakers and seamstresses. Needle skills for women were highly regarded in those days, and along with sewing the girls learned knitting and crocheting. Predating Rosie Greer by many decades (Rosie Greer was the football star of the '60s who relaxed by creating and stitching his own needlepoint), I had a real interest in knitting and crocheting. To learn how this art form was done, I often joined the girls in their classroom. While the main reason to join the girls was to learn needlework, the secondary reason was the girls themselves. I had sisters, but these girls were different.

First, they weren't my sisters, and second, they were, almost to a girl, absolutely beautiful. I just loved being with them, but there was one girl in particular with whom I was totally infatuated. This was my second infatuation, and I couldn't keep my eyes off her. She was pretty, was kind to everyone and she smelled nice, something all the boys noticed and commented upon. But none of us got to first base with her. Maybe because we were all shy and being in her presence made tongues go into knots. I know mine did. I could talk a blue streak with my sisters, but this girl made me go stupid. It would be many years before I would have a girlfriend that wasn't just in my dreams.

After Boris Ginodman, the new director of the Orthodox home was Mme. Krakofski, a super-Orthodox woman, who prior to coming to Eaubonne, had taught at a French boy's school, the Ecole Maimonides, in Bois de Boulogne.

Mme. Krakofski was a tough taskmaster who demanded strict discipline. Believing the only way to learn a language was total immersion, she refused to speak to us in either German or Yiddish—both in or out of the classroom—and insisted that we speak to her only in French.

Mme. Krakofski considered us an unruly bunch and took it upon herself to instill discipline. Not used to rules and regulations that were now being imposed by mademoiselle, many of the students felt that she was too strict, and soon rebellion was in the air. After several weeks, a group of boys, some of the oldest and most rowdy, rioted. Mme. Krakofski's room was broken into and ransacked. Her bed was smashed and thrown into the corridor and the contents of a chest of drawers and a closet were emptied and strewn all over the room.

While many of the other boys joined in with little encouragement, to my credit, I didn't. But, to my shame, I didn't try to stop it, either. I was especially ashamed when the bed sheets that had been thrown into the hallway showed evidences of blood. At this stage of my life, I knew nothing of menstruation, and I was filled with a horror and embarrassment that could only have been a hundred times worse for Mme. Krakofski. I will never forgive myself for not standing up to the bullies to try to make them stop.

In the aftermath, Ernst Papanek was summoned to restore civil order. We were all called together in an assembly, and he gave us the worst tongue-lashing we had ever had. While the ringleaders were punished, in my estimation, it was a mild punishment, probably because the faculty, as well as Mme. Krakofski herself, realized that she really had been way too strict. First, we were just kids. More than that, we were kids who had no home, no parents, no family. Many didn't know where their parents or siblings were, or even if they were alive. Life had dealt us a lousy hand, and we didn't need more stress from our teacher.

From that time on, she relaxed and became more mellow. The result was that we all began to respect her. With her new attitude, we even began to like her. It was especially gratifying to the little ones who didn't speak French when she would address them in either Yiddish or German. With everything in their world being strange and new, the smaller children didn't need one more unfamiliarity to upset their young lives. A small comfort, perhaps, but a comfort it was for many to be able to communicate in the language in which they were raised.

I was becoming a language expert. I knew German and French by this time and now I was learning Yiddish. Coming from a small town in Germany, I had never heard Yiddish spoken before. Not all Jews spoke Yiddish, a language that was more prevalently spoken by Jews in central and Eastern Europe. It is a language that has appropriated words from Hebrew, old German, and any of the country's languages in which the Yiddish speakers resided. To my ears it sounded like very bad German, but I soon learned otherwise because many of the kids at the home came from Eastern European families where Yiddish was spoken, and I soon learned to appreciate its color and nuance.

In 1939, Hitler decreed that no Jew could practice as a dentist, veterinarian or chemist, and all other Jewish enterprises were closed. In a session of the German parliament, Hitler publicly revealed his plan to exterminate all European Jews. Membership in the Hitler Youth was now mandatory for all non-Jewish German youth, and the Ravenstock concentration camp was opened in northern Germany to accommodate Jewish women. Jewish women now shared the same fate as Jewish men.

As I look back, I'm certain our teachers from the OSE and ORT knew more than they were telling us about what was happening in Germany and the world. We were shielded from knowing the worst of it and were kept occupied with our studies. I still didn't fear for my mother and sisters. I imagined them as I last saw them; murdering women was beyond my power to imagine. And I had proof that they were well. I had received letters from them that indicated they were safe at the old age home, a place we were later to learn the Nazis purposely kept open to assemble Jews who had been rounded up or arrested. The old age home was to become the first step to the concentration camps.

When we weren't in school, like children everywhere, we were busy with recreational activities and sports. Ball games were organized, and teams were chosen with the favorite being *Voelkerball*, the German form of dodge ball. I was pretty athletic, especially in Voelkerball and was always one of the first to be picked to be part of a team.

Then there was the perennial favorite sport: soccer. The OSE prepared several playing fields for the appropriate sports with soccer being the most prominent. For indoor activities, we had a Ping-Pong table, of which I was particularly proficient, and card games galore.

We also made up our own games. One such game was a really popular game called "Horse," which we boys love to play. The older and larger boys became the horse, and smaller kids would sit on the horse's shoulders. The idea was to dismount your opponent; the game had few rules of play so it was a game that could get rough.

Part of our education was learning to govern ourselves as well as abide by the rules, so a *Heimrat* (student council) was initiated. It was decided that only three people would be elected as representatives: Ernst Valver, Friedel Chanalas and I were voted in.

Our first disciplinary cases involved two or three boys who were rambunctious, loud and rowdy enough to warrant discipline. Found guilty, a jury was selected to decide on the punishment for their infractions. The punishment always was appropriate for the infraction.

In another case, one of the bigger boys was found guilty of bullying some of the smaller girls and another boy. As his punishment he was placed in a wooden barrel and rolled down the street for 15 minutes. A bit bruised by the rough interior of the barrel, I don't think he ever picked on the little kids again. Perhaps that would be a good form of punishment for classroom bullies today.

The arts were important, and I remember that a number of my classmates were highly artistic, whether in creating beautiful pictures, beautiful music or putting words together to create stories or poems. One boy, who was a year older than me, was a gifted poet as well as being blessed with a keen sense of humor. For each one of us in the dorm, he composed a funny poem giving everybody a silly nickname. Benno Singer, who always had feet that smelled like Limburger cheese, was nicknamed Kaese (cheese). My name was Batsch, because I was short and stocky. The nicknames stuck, and 40 years later at a Los Angeles reunion of kids from the French school, I heard my nickname, Batsch, called out from across the room. Even after all those years, we were still calling each other by the nicknames that creative little boy had given us.

CHAPTER
NINE

"Heinz, is that you?" the man implored. In a long dark coat that seemed out of place for the season, he looked old and stooped, but he continued to look penetratingly into my eyes as if trying to find someone else's face there. It was the middle of May, and I was on the ball field with my friends. His appearance half annoyed me. He had just made me fumble the ball. But there was something about him that was familiar. Looking at him more closely I recognized Uncle Isador Marks, the man from the orphanage who refused to report to Hitler's concentration camp, and who escaped to Palestine chaperoning the passage of 35 Jewish children from Germany.

"What are *you* doing here?" I cried, ever so happy to see him.

"It's a very long story, Heinz," he said, his eyes blinking rapidly. I have been in Palestine, but I missed my home. I was on my way back to my home in Frankfurt and to resume my duties at the orphanage when someone I knew found me and gave me a message. That message said I was not to go there. I don't know who sent the message—the messenger wouldn't tell me—or he didn't know. But he was adamant that I should not go to Frankfurt because the Nazis were still looking for me. If they found me, I don't know what they would do, arrest me for sure and probably kill me like so many others. It isn't safe for me in Germany, so I am trying to get to England. My children are there, and I want to be with them. It's been too long without my children. My home now is with my children."

He spent two days with me before he continued his journey to England to be reunited with his son and daughter. It was wonderful to talk to him, to giggle over funny things that happened at the home. Reminiscing with him made it all come alive again. Teachers and counselors who were, as we spoke of them, possibly dead in Hitler's gas chambers, still laughed, still danced and led normal lives as we, one by one, brought their memory back to life. But, too soon he was gone—on the next leg of his journey and once he was gone the reality of the present crushed in on me again. I, too, was a long way from the orphanage in Frankfurt and an even longer way from my real home in Sterbfritz. I was in yet another orphanage, still away from my family and alone. I longed for my mother and sisters. I ached to go home to the way it was. I tried to will myself back in time and make it all come alive, but I couldn't, and it didn't. I cried myself to sleep, again hating the weakness in me.

Germany attacked Poland on September 1, 1939, and France and England declared war on Germany two days later. Now, German Jews were forbidden to be outdoors after 8 p.m. in the winter and 9 p.m. in the summer. On September 23, 1939, German Jews were forbidden to own a radio, and Dër Stürmer, the Nazi newspaper, declared, "The Jewish people ought to be exterminated root and branch. Then the plague of pests would have disappeared in Poland at one stroke."

We knew that declaration of war on Germany by France would result in retaliation against the Jews and probably by air attack. Our fear was that Germany would bomb places known to be Jewish hideouts so preparations were made to find safe shelters for the children in case this is what they did.

The largest room in the Villa Chesnaie's basement was turned into an air raid shelter. Electric light was installed, and enough benches were placed there to accommodate all the children and adults. We were told that in case of an air raid, sirens would sound, and we were absolutely not to turn on any lights other than in the air raid shelter itself. Several of the older boys and girls were appointed air raid wardens to make sure orders were carried out as given.

We had air raid drills almost daily, and we knew exactly what to do if there was an air attack, or God forbid, a poison gas attack. We were ready. We were told that in case of a gas attack to soak our handkerchief in vinegar and place it over our nose and mouth and a large tub with vinegar was placed in the entryway of the so-called air raid shelter. The vinegar was supposed to filter out the poisonous gas. Later, we were issued gas masks.

We were also warned not to pick up edibles, especially candy, if we found it on the ground outside. I don't know if it was true, but all children, French and foreign children, were told not to touch it. Candy found on the ground could have been dropped by German planes, and if so, it was poisoned.

Poisoned candy was only one of the hazards we feared we might encounter. Some of the younger boys were exploring the grounds of the villa and found artillery shells. Panic broke out because if there were German artillery shells, could Germans be far away? French authorities were summoned to examine the shells, but they determined that the ammunition was left over from World War I and was totally harmless. As we now know, they might not have been harmless even after all those years. But the French authorities removed them, no one was injured and calm was restored.

"All things considered, the children followed their instructions remarkably well. Except for one thing. Many of them either forgot to put on the shoes and coats which had been so carefully laid out ahead of time or bolted out of the room without bothering to. But that was all right. Each home had elected two

representatives to the Children's Parliament, and these student leaders were responsible for going from room to room with two of the teachers to collect the clothing that had been left behind. Most instructional. It was cold in those cellars in the early fall mornings. While the offenders were shivering in their pajamas, they could also shiver at the thought that they were placing the people they most admired in unnecessary danger. After that first night, no child ever forgot his clothing again."— 'Out of the Fire" by Ernst Papanek with Edward Linn*

In early October, we heard the sirens and loud booms from the ack-ack guns. Ack-ack guns were a type of anti-aircraft artillery. All the drills, all the instruction now came into play. This was the real thing. We could hear the guns and planes overhead, and it all seemed so frightening. But soon we heard the drone of the attack planes get fainter as they retreated into the smoke-filled skies. The first attack was over, and when the all clear sounded we each were given a small chocolate bar to pacify us and told to go back to bed.

The next morning, several French police officers and soldiers came to the home. A German flier had been shot down and was not found immediately. Interestingly, the authorities figured that because we were German we could be hiding the flier. Though we were Jewish refugees who had fled Germany, strangely they figured our loyalties were still with the Fatherland.

Time and time again, the sirens sounded and time and time again we went to the air raid shelter. During the air raids, which sometimes lasted hours, there was nothing to do, so we often talked, even if in a whisper, to pass the time.

Once, I sat next to Ernst Valfer, whose parents were opera buffs and who passed the love for the art form on to their son. In the shelter, Ernst practically recited verbatim the libretto of numerous operas he had attended with his parents. The stories were wonderful—mostly about a handsome man infatuated with a beautiful maiden, whether she was a princess (Turandot), a priestess (Lakmé or The Pearl Fishers), a girl who worked in a cigarette factory (Carmen) or a starving artist in love with a girl who made artificial flowers (La Bohème). I loved all the stories and was fascinated with the imagery. When I was able to hear for myself the music and singing, opera and classical music became my passion for the rest of my life.

After October, routine was restored, and it was almost as if there was no war raging in Europe. The only tangible evidence that the war was still on was that all direct mail to and from Germany and Austria had stopped. To communicate with my family in Germany, I had to send my letters to a family member in Switzerland who would then forward the mail from me to Germany and mail from Germany to me. It took weeks for a letter to get through if it did at all. For some time now, there had been no word from my mother or sisters, nor were they mentioned in letters from other family members. Because I was kept so busy with my studies, sports and chores, I had little time to think about what might have happened to my mother and sisters. Life went on.

Life went on and chores had to be done. Several of us had bakery duty, that is, the responsibility to go to the bakery in Eaubonne to pick up bread for the home. It was a "chore" we all volunteered to do because the bakery was olfactory heaven, smelling so delicious we could almost taste the bread from the smell in the air. Once we picked up the loaves, it was our responsibility to take them back to the home, but on several occasions we couldn't resist the lure of the freshly baked bread. There were so many loaves, we figured no one would notice the two or three loaves that we had poked through the crust with our fingers to get to the deliciously hot, soft bread inside. For two or three trips, we got away with our deception, but we were eventually discovered. Hollow loaves of bread raised red flags with the administrators, and it wasn't hard to find "whodunit." How long we got away with it, I don't remember. But once discovered, I decided that it was better to buy a baguette or two for myself with the few francs that I had. If I paid for it, I got to eat the fresh bread and didn't get in trouble.

I made the baguettes I bought for myself last several days. But, even though I hid them, one of my bunkmates must have seen my hiding place and he stole the baguettes I was saving for later.

"Who stole my baguettes?" I cried, near tears with outrage. Silence was the only answer, and I couldn't help think everyone knew. I never had proof of who the culprit was, but I think it was Ernst Marks, one of the six boys who bunked in my room. Ernst was an odd duck, always telling wild stories about all the great things he had done, and he always seemed angry about something. At 15, he was still a bed wetter. Looking back, I know Ernst had emotional problems and was to be pitied, but at the time I just hated him. I went into a depression for days, frustrated by the unfairness and because there was nothing I could do to get even.

The battles still raged, but we had other worries more immediate than the war and stolen baguettes. During the winter of 1939-1940, sickness of all sorts was rampant and France experienced an outbreak of diphtheria. Dr. Helena Papanek made sure all the children from the three homes were vaccinated, much to our displeasure. Not only did the shots hurt, but most of our Eaubonne group reacted to the vaccine and came down with a high fever that lasted two or three days. Those of us who had no reaction were pressed into service nursing the sick, feeding them in bed and sponging them with cool water to bring down the fever. We also had to help them to the bathroom, brush their teeth and keep them in clean pajamas. It was hard work, but I know they would have done it for me. Besides, it felt good to help others.

Almost as quickly as it hit, the diphtheria crisis was over and we resumed our ordinary lives. The war again seemed distant and boys being boys, my friend Fred and I longed for adventure. Adventure then was to scrounge around the unused portion of the basement, a place where we thought nobody could find us. While down there one day, we found a tin box with a lid and also a bag of either plaster or cement. For posterity, we decided to bury two chocolate bars that we got during an air raid in the metal box. We encased the box in a mixture of cement and sand, properly prepared it with water and buried it in the most remote area of the grounds. Then, we drew a map of the location so that in lean times we could find our treasure. We never went back, and the chocolate bars may still be there.

Our teachers and counselors knew we were growing up without family memories and that it would be easy to forget the people who loved us most. To keep our relationships alive, they encouraged us to write letters home. In fact, weekly letter-writing times were established for the younger boys and girls. I was a lazy writer, and my family in Germany had often complained in their letters to me about my sparse writing. But, I was a boy, and life was good. I had lots of playmates and more things to do than I could possible have the time to do. Sitting still to write letters was more than I could fathom. If I had had more maturity (or a glimpse into what the future would hold) I would have taken letter writing more seriously. If I had known that I would soon embark on a lifetime without them, I would have cherished any communication I could get—in any form I could get it. But, I didn't know.

On April 27, 1940, Himmler issued a directive to establish a concentration camp for Jews in Auschwitz. On May 10, 1940, the French government surrendered to the German army and an armistice was signed. British troops in northern France fled to the English Channel at Dunkirk where most, along with many French soldiers, were rescued and taken back to England. With the British military gone, there was nothing to stop the German army from heading straight toward Paris.

"May 10, 1940, was a beautiful morning."—"Out of the Fire" *by Ernst Papanek with Edward Linn*

On June 7, 1940, German troops were poised to enter Paris. While we knew about it, we trusted our caregivers so completely we were not panicked. However, I was to learn later that the Papaneks were highly concerned about the safety of the children in all three homes and they decided to move all the children from the various homes and bring them together in one place. In case of attack, it would be easier to protect us if we were all together, and if evacuation was required, time would not be wasted rounding us up.

Mr. Papanek thought the children should know what was going on so maps were drawn and arrows placed on the maps showing where the German troops were invading. We all knew the seriousness of the situation, and everyone pulled their weight as preparations for evacuation began. Each child was given a survival bag that held essentials like socks, toothbrushes and toothpaste, pajamas and even a small bar of chocolate. The bag was kept next to the bed alongside our gas mask and clothing. In the event of a night departure, it could be grabbed quickly and easily.

We evacuated in groups of four or six, driven by car through the streets already crowded with tanks and French military personnel who showed great empathy for us. At checkpoints, they often joked with us, put their helmets on our heads and told us we could touch their rifles, thereby making them seem less scary. Guns were everywhere, and we got used to seeing them.

Finally, we reached the train station, and we boarded a train from Paris to Limoges. From Limoges, we were bused to the Chateau Montintin, a remote location approximately 20 kilometers from the train station. It was a place I was later to learn was chosen because of its remoteness.

All of the children were evacuated in this way and not one was lost. Looking back, it was a miracle that the OSE was able to pull it off because not all of the older kids could go with us in the first groups that left the home. All boys and girls 16 years or older were not allowed to accompany the rest of us because the French government required older children to have special travel papers. They had to go separately.

We were all concerned for their safety and rightly so because they were to face dangers we didn't have to face, dangers we could only imagine. But about four or five days later, a truck arrived with all of the stragglers. We were jubilant, yelling, laughing and jumping up and down. When calm was restored, they told us how harrowing it all had been.

They said the exodus from Paris to unoccupied France was mayhem. The roads out of Paris were a crush of people on foot and bicycles as well as cars, trucks and horse carts. Everyone who was able to walk, ride a bicycle or procure a vehicle tried to escape the Nazi onslaught. The gasoline shortage resulted in a glut of cars that had run out of gas and had to be pushed out of the road onto the shoulder to keep the way open. The people who walked carried bulging suitcases and duffle bags. Bed clothes with treasured possessions tied inside were slung over stooped shoulders. The Nazis tried to stop the mass exodus by strafing the crowds from low-flying aircraft. Many people were gunned down in the roads and the streets; blood and bodies were everywhere. Children sat silently next to the dead bodies of their parents. It was hell.

But our teenagers and young adults were saved by somehow getting a truck with a full tank of gas, which one of the adult teachers was able to drive to the train station. In that way, they were able to join the rest of the group. Our prayers had been answered—they were with us, and they were safe.

Accompanying the younger children on the train were Frau Kanner, Mme. Krakofski (she was a French citizen), and an older student who evidently already had her travel papers. The shoemaker, Eagen, stayed behind and came later with another one of the boys. I don't remember what became of Leon, the Polish communist who lived with us at the Villa Chesnaie. However, Frau Kanner's husband was interned at Gurs. A small contingent went to Brout Vernet near Vichy. Our group that had been so happy living in Villa Chesnaie, was slowly breaking apart, and the harsh reality of the war crept again into our consciousness.

We were tired and hungry when we arrived at Chateau Montintin, a place we found to be an ancient castle that had been modified, though not entirely updated, throughout the years. There was no furniture in the main house or in the old servants' quarters known as the *chevrette*, which was up a hill from the main house, so we had to improvise.

The chevrette had three floors. The first floor was to be our kitchen and dining room. The second floor became the boys' bedrooms, and the third floor became the girls' rooms. The chevrette's toilet facility was a primitive outhouse located by the stables several yards from our living quarters. It was rustic and inconvenient by today's standards, but somehow it didn't take long before we were accustomed to traipsing outdoors to go to the bathroom. We began to acclimate to our new surroundings. What was important was that we were all together.

To make the castle seem more homelike, we Orthodox kids moved to the chevrette, and brought our Safer Torah and religious articles with us. Familiar things surrounding us created a sense of wellbeing.

The kitchen was the first thing to be set up. I remember watching a group of peasant women who were hired to slaughter and dress domestic rabbits for our first meal. Seeing the manner in which they prepared the hares was appalling. Nothing was done in a kosher manner. We who were raised by our parents to be religiously observant had a choice to make: either eat the nonkosher rabbits or eat food we called *tobinambour* (horrible-tasting fodder food). I chose the horrible tasting fodder food. That first night, my friend, Dudu, and I found a discarded basket of wormy cherries. We were so hungry, we didn't care. We ate the cherries along with the worms. It seemed more right than to eat what was religiously forbidden.

We had no beds, so the first several days we slept on the hard floor. A cabinetry shop was set up almost immediately in the former stables, but until furniture could be made we fabricated makeshift tables and benches to be used in the dining rooms for both the main house and the chevrette.

It wasn't very long before the OSE somehow managed to retrieve our beds from the three former homes. In retrospect, the OSE accomplished miracles to get us to safety into unoccupied France and further accomplished miracles in providing for us as well as they did. They were miracle workers.

When all necessary furniture was built, we turned our attention to making the chateau look more homey so we made art objects by using veneers and several species of hardwood. I, myself, made my first chessboard. At that age, I wasn't interested in reading books or studying. However, I was good with my hands, and I loved woodworking—making beautiful things from shapeless pieces of wood. Something from nothing.

Several of the older boys volunteered to work with the local foresters, learning how to fell trees then cut them into logs. I volunteered to go with them. It was hard work, but I enjoyed every minute of it. Our reward was getting several loaves of bread every day, a larger ration than the other kids got but much of it we willingly shared with the other kids.

When we weren't out cutting down trees, we were working in the woodshop, a job I loved but one that could be dangerous. Once, when I was cutting a board for a dresser, sawdust blew into my eye.

It hurt so much tears ran down my face. My first thought was that my eye would fall out, and I remember holding my hand in a cup fashion under my eye hoping to catch it before it fell to the ground. It must have been funny to my friend Boris because he laughed until he was crying too. Finally getting his mirth under control, he assured me that I wouldn't lose my eye, but it had to stop hurting and my vision had come back before I believed him.

To be my friend, Boris sometimes put up with a great deal from me. Once, he wasn't so good-natured, and I made him mad. I was using the grindstone wheel to sharpen a chisel when Boris walked up behind me and asked me to show him what I was doing. When I turned abruptly toward him, I accidentally cut him with the sharpened tool. Reflexively, he slapped me, hard, almost knocking me down. We were both mad, but walked away from each other. "It was an accident," I yelled at his back. "I didn't mean to harm you," I screamed. Later, after we both cooled off, he apologized. I was so grateful he said he was sorry. Boris was my friend, and I didn't want to lose him, especially since I was beginning to think it really had been my fault.

For the most part, we were able to ignore the war, often instances would occur that brought us back to reality. I recall that after a few days in Montintin all of us from the main house and the chevrette were assembled in a large room on the second floor. All those who spoke French were told to sit on the floor immediately inside the door. French authorities and a German officer waited for us to file in and once assembled asked us questions. Our teachers and counselors wanted the French-speaking children closest to the German officer so that any questions would be directed at them. We didn't know if they knew there were German, Austrian and Polish Jewish children present, and our counselors thought it best to conceal the fact if possible. Satisfied that there was no problem at the home, they left as quickly as they came, but our nerves were shattered.

Ernst Papanek and family arrived at Montintin a few days after we did only to say goodbye. They wanted to see us one last time to explain why they could not stay with us any longer. They told us they were political undesirables (though not Communists, they were avowed socialists) and therefore the Nazi government thought they were a threat. Even then, the Nazis were looking for them, and if found they would be sent to a concentration camp along with the Jews.

As children, we didn't understand the seriousness of their situation, and many of us felt they had abandoned us. Looking back, I understand they had done all they could to help us, and others would now take over. The Papaneks' presence would only have drawn Nazi attention to us, and if they had stayed, we might all have been killed. They had made a tough, but wise, decision.

So the Papaneks, along with their two boys, fled to Spain, then to Portugal where they boarded a Boeing Yankee 314 clipper and made the trans-Atlantic flight to New York.

Food was scarce now, and we boys who did the lion's share of physical labor were always hungry. In kindness, many of the girls shared their rations with the us. Kosher meat was available only once a week from Limoges, but it didn't last long. We made do with what was available.

Fortunately, there was an apple orchard close to the house. The apples had been harvested, but many were left on the ground or still hanging on the branches. Those we picked with relish and ate as many as our stomachs could hold. Not only did we preserve the apples, I had the brainstorm that we could make cider. My scavenging paid off. In the far corner of the attic, I found a sack with about 30 bottles. The bottles had self-closing tops, and I thought that these might come in handy for making cider.

My mother used to make cider and vinegar every year from the apples in our orchard, so I had seen her do it. I remember seeing her squeeze the apples and put the juice into bottles for fermentation, but I guess I didn't watch her closely enough. Dudu, Fred and I used bench vises to squeeze the apples. We washed the bottles and filled 10 to 20 of them, carefully putting the self-closing caps on each bottle. That was our big mistake. After several weeks in the attic, fermentation began; as the cider expanded it had no place to go. One by one, the bottles exploded. It was a mess I'll never forget.

I think as a youngster I was a disaster waiting to happen. Other catastrophes happened to me as well like the notorious glue-pot incident. Before the days of white and yellow glue, all wood glues were made of animal compounds. The glue in the pot had to be liquefied by heating it on a stove, and at the end of the day the pot was removed from the stove allowing it to cool and again solidify. Once, when one of my co-apprentices was using the glue, he knocked the glue pot off the stove, glue splattering all over the floor and all over my leg. It hurt, and I couldn't scrape it off my leg fast enough. But even if I had been able to scrape it all off, it was too late. I had severe burns all over my leg. The wounds were so bad that in a few days they became infected, and I remember I was bedridden for days as well as semi-delirious with fever. I still have the scars.

Another time, I was chosen to fetch milk from a local farmer for what we called milk soup, that is, milk diluted with water to make it go farther and served for breakfast. Several of us older boys had the task of going by bicycle every evening to pick up the milk can for breakfast the next morning. We'd sling the can's handle over the handlebars, which freed both hands to hold on.

That night, it was my turn to fetch the milk, and I though how fortunate it was that there was a full moon. I picked up the milk and adjusted the cans on the handlebars so they would ride well and started out. On the way home, I took a path I had taken before, so I knew it pretty well. But this night, the moon cast shadows across the road, and at a bend in the road I mistook a moon shadow for a tree that had fallen across the way. I braked so hard the bike came to an immediate stop. Unfortunately, I didn't, and I went head over heels across the handle bars. The milk cans flew, splattering milk all over the ground. I knew I was in trouble, so I went back to the farm house to ask for more milk. While they commiserated with my plight, they couldn't give me more because they didn't have more. I felt so guilty that when I arrived back at the chevrette I cried and tried to explain what happened. With so little to eat, we didn't need wasted milk. Kind soul that she was, Frau Kanner hugged me to try to make me feel better, but I didn't. I knew I blew it. I knew I had let them all down.

CHAPTER

TEN

In 1941, Hitler reaffirmed his goal to rid the world of all Jews. As in Germany, in occupied France, Jews were prohibited from owning stores or businesses and were forbidden to do business with gentiles. Jewish ghettos were established in Czestoclowa, Krakow, Lublin, Radom and Kielce in Poland and Danica, Laborgrad, Jadovna, Gradiska and Djakovo in Croatia. The Warsaw Ghetto held 400,000 people, and in March, 70,000 more were added to that number. The Nazis allowed ghetto inhabitants an amount of food that totaled only 183 calories per day.

Sometime in April of 1941, a rumor spread throughout both houses at Montintin that the United States would accept refugee children from France. Shortly after, the announcement was made official. At that time, no one knew who was to be picked, and everyone was anxious.

Around the first of May, the list of those who would be on the first transport was posted. My name, as well as the 10 others who came to France from Frankfurt, were chosen. Three of our Frankfurt group who had been sent to Brout Vernet near Vichy were also on the list. At the time, I was only aware of the single transport, but I found out years later at a refugee reunion in New

York that there had actually been a second and a third transport, and more kids than I knew were able to escape war-torn Europe.

On May 18, 1941, we left Montintin for Marseille to report to the American consulate where we stayed until June 1. I remember I was frightened. When we were at the home, it was easy to forget what was happening in the world outside and just be kids. But now, the reality was again in our faces. We saw Nazi soldiers with guns, German tanks with swastikas and bombed-out buildings. What happened while we were waiting to leave is all a blur. I don't remember how we were billeted or how we got our meals. Some tell me I don't remember because the time was so frightening that I blocked it out of my memory. That could be, but I do remember that on June 1 we left by train for Spain and Portugal with a stop at the internment camp at Gurs. When the train pulled into the station, several kids from our transport recognized their parents in the crowd and were able to get off the train for a few brief minutes to be with them. It was the last time most of them would see them, for Gurs was shortly thereafter converted from an internment camp to a concentration camp, a camp that would have few survivors.

Once we arrived at the Spanish border, we were transferred from the French train to a Spanish train. I'll never forget the view out the train window as we crossed the Great Pyrenees Mountains. I had never seen such stark, majestic beauty. The snow pack had not yet melted, and for miles all we could see was a sparkling white blanket that covered the land.

The train had several individual passenger cars and several freight cars. Compartments in the passenger cars housed about six people each. Somehow, I managed to be in the same compartment with the beautiful Elfriede. We were both more frightened than we had ever been, but I think she comforted me more than I comforted her. I remember I slept part of both nights with my head in her lap.

The rest of the time, I hid in the wooden luggage rack suspended from the ceiling over the benches.

As the train climbed steeper up into the mountains, it felt like the steam engine was gasping to get to the summit, and I was afraid she wouldn't make it. That night, I dreamed the train got stuck in the snow and there was no hope for rescue. Sitting upright, I awoke from the nightmare drenched in sweat. It seems death was always around the corner whether I was awake or asleep.

When daybreak came, I could tell the engine had made it to the top for it had quit laboring, and we were now descending. It was a relief when we saw Spain, even if some of what we saw was ugly reminders of the bloody Spanish Civil War and revolution of 1936-1939. Railroad beds had been blown up along with the engines and rail cars; abandoned vehicles were everywhere as well as abandoned cannon, machine guns and other kinds of military equipment—all in various states of rust.

We arrived in Madrid on June 2, and from the station we were transported to a Catholic convent to spend the night. There, we got our first hot meal in days. I'll never forget it. It was macaroni with tomato sauce. It was delicious!

But tensions were high and arguments over petty things started between some of the kids in our group. One area of contention was Catholic religious figures in the convent. Our evening prayers were conducted in a room that had crosses and Catholic religious statues. Two of the boys insisted the idolatrous items be removed from the room. Judaism has no religious figures because of the fear that people might begin to worship the figures instead the God they represent. My argument, and the argument of most of the others, was that we were guests of these people and had no right to remove anything. We won, and we conducted our services under the plaster statues of Jesus and the Virgin Mary.

The next day, June 3, we continued on our way to Lisbon by way of Valencia. Upon our arrival, we were greeted with gifts of oranges and chocolates presented to us by a lovely Portuguese-Jewish woman and several others. We stayed there over night; they had made room for us in a Portuguese school. We loved Spain and would have been happy to remain there, basking in the Spanish sunshine and filling ourselves with fabulous Spanish food. But all too soon we had to move on, and on June 10, we boarded the Portuguese freighter Mouzinho, a cargo ship that sometimes transported passengers.

I remember they told us the Mouzinho's hold was filled with cork, but this trip she also carried 100 children as well as a number of adult Jewish refugees. I was told one of the passengers was a world-renowned violinist by the name of Rubinoff, a Russian-born musician who, I believe, went on to become a well-known artist.

Steerage was converted to accommodate all 100 kids as well as the adults. Men, women, girls and boys were all cramped into this hold, but luckily we were allowed to go topside for fresh air.

The sea was rough and the trip was arduous; most everybody got seasick, a malady to which I didn't succumb, thank G-d. I felt no ill effects of the rough sea though often the waves washed up on deck and we had to be careful not to get washed overboard.

Dudu and I, the explorers, often went to the engine compartment where we volunteered to help shovel coal into the boiler. The Portuguese firemen were delighted and invited us to come every day if we wanted, happy to have such cheap labor and glad to sit back and watch us do the work. In payment, they always had something nice for us to eat. I don't remember if the food was kosher, and I don't think we cared. It was delicious, and we ate it gratefully.

The voyage lasted 11 days, and rumor had it that the Mouzinho was being followed by a German submarine. One of the boys swore he saw the sub surface every evening, but none of the rest of us ever saw it. We docked on Staten Island early in the morning on June 21. America at last! Safe at last!

CHAPTER
ELEVEN

Before leaving Montintin, we were given a farewell talk that closed with the thought: "When you see the Statue of Liberty, think of France during better times." We passed the grand lady early in the morning on June 21, 1941. I remember how I thought of those parting words, and they confused me because I had no knowledge that in 1886 the Statue of Liberty had been a gift from France to the United States. But, I remembered to think of France in better times anyway.

As the S.S. Mouzinho's engines came to an almost complete stop, we saw a small boat approach the ship. Someone told us that the small boat was a pilot boat, or a tugboat, that would steer the Mouzinho into Staten Island harbor. All this meant nothing to me; I had no idea what was happening. All I cared about was that we were in America. My eyes couldn't see enough.

I was on the top deck watching as the ship was maneuvered into its berth when someone told me a man was looking for Heinz Schuster. I ran to see who it was and immediately recognized my cousin Norbert Braunschweiger waving frantically at me from the dock. I was dumbfounded. So much had been orchestrated without

1939

Rosa Schuster

Abraham Schuster

Henry, flanked by his two sisters:
Margot on the left and Bertel on the right.

Henry Schuster (age 13) with his mother Rosa, and sister, Bertel.

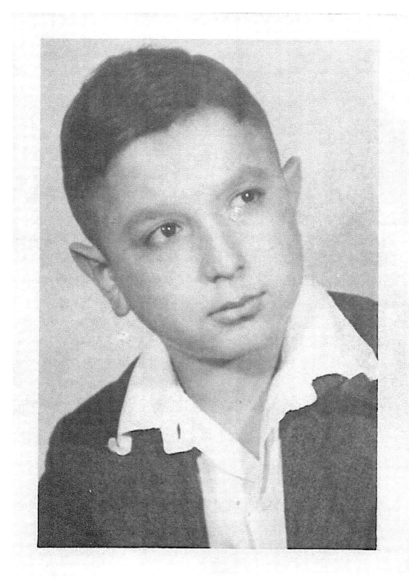

Henry Schuster at age 12.

Zerstörtes Gebäude, aufgenommen von einem amerikanischen Soldaten, der mit einem Kindertransport aus dem Waisenhaus nach Frankreich gerettet wurde, 1946
Henry Schuster, Las Vegas

**The Waisenhaus (orphanage)
where Henry was to spend several years.**

Paris -46-

Henry Schuster and sister, Bertel,
shortly after being reunited in Paris.

Abraham Schuster's headstone in Altengronau cemetery.

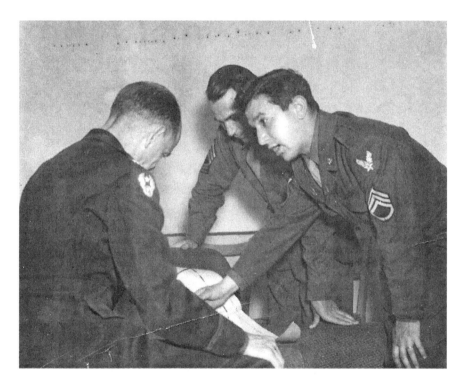

Henry confers with his superior officers on plans for the new enlisted men's club in Ansbach, Germany.

Henry Schuster's Adolf Hitler impersonation.

Anita and Henry on Anita's 17th birthday in 1947.

**Prom night 1947—Anita Kleiman and Henry Schuster.
Anita would later become Mrs. Henry Schuster.**

Mature trees now populate Altengronau Jewish cemetery.

Plaque memorializing the Sterbfritz Jews who died
at the hands of the Nazis during WWII was erected
and dedicated on March 30, 2004.

The following is a translation of the German text on the memorial stone erected in the Sterbfritz Cemetery.

Remember!
These are the names of the Jewish men, women and children who were murdered in the National Socialist extermination camps.

NAME	DATE OF BIRTH
Abraham Birk	9/03/1862
Michael Birk	28/02/1872
Frieda Birk	16/03/1876
Georg Fries	18/07/1913
Josef Goldschmidt	12/03/1865
Abraham Goldschmidt	28/07/1876
Amalie Goldschmidt	09/04/1871
Felix Goldschmidt	28/07/1876
Malchen Goldschmidt	22/04/1881
Max Hecht	14/08/1881
Lina Hecht	01/06/1887
Meir Hecht	27/12/1885
Gitta Hecht	20/07/1890
Ludwig Hecht	26/07/1923
Sofie Hecht	02/09/1926
Jacob Hecht	20/03/1884

Else Hecht	24/12/1895
Lother Hecht	13/09/1923
Steffi Hecht	12/11/1927
Lazurus Hecht	15/07/1875
Leopold Kahn	12/05/1872
Hanchen Kahn	26/10/1873
Berta Kahn	15/09/1907
Moritz Mansbach	28/08/1881
Lea Mansbach	08/04/1882
Aron Marx	19/11/1881
Betti Marx	27/02/1881
Marta Neuhaus	03/07/1907
Rosa Schuster	12/06/1891
Margot Schuster	18/10/1922
Emma Schuster	23/09/1877

We commemorate them and remember the immeasurable suffering of those who were persecuted and murdered. May their fate be an appeal to the living for peace and tolerance.

Peace!

our knowledge. I didn't know that any of my relatives in the United States knew of my whereabouts. I barely knew I *had* any relatives in the United States.

Upon debarking, Norbert and his new wife ran up to greet me. I didn't know Norbert was in New York, but I was later to discover that he had relatives in Shreveport, Louisiana who sponsored *his* emigration. On the ship to America, he met the woman who was to become his bride.

Beside them was a man I didn't recognize and who, it turned out, was my cousin Milan Schuster from Sterbfritz. Milan's wife, Mina, had relatives in Ohio who sent money so that they could buy their way out of Germany. Norbert and Milan hugged me so hard my feet came off the ground, and they whirled me around and around. I was overcome with embarrassment that I didn't recognize my cousin, but he assured me the last time I had seen him I was just a little boy so I shouldn't be embarrassed. But I was embarrassed all the same because I must have seen him and his daughter, Ina, every day. Ina and I were the same age and had been playmates. How could I have forgotten? Some of the other kids had relatives greeting them as well and to our surprise, the Papaneks were also there. They had made it out of Europe safely and on to New York. I was so happy to see them because I had been worried sick about them. Everyone was talking at once, and the hubbub was overwhelming. We felt like celebrities because in addition to the grand greeting from our families, there must have been a dozen newspaper and magazine reporters trying to get interviews and taking pictures.

When we were finally able to get free, we found that several buses were standing by to transport us into the city. Once everyone was on board, the buses were driven onto a ferry that crossed to Manhattan. The excitement mounted as we drew nearer to the shore, and we couldn't wait to arrive at our destination, a Jewish children's home on Amsterdam Avenue and 37th Street.

Several German-speaking men and women welcomed us and helped us with our meager belongings. A bigger surprise was that my Uncle Salli (my mother's brother) was part of the welcoming committee. Uncle Salli, who had been a prosperous hardware store merchant in Josbach, now worked as a janitor, a job he was glad to get because with limited English language skills new immigrants found it hard to find employment. They took whatever work they could find. Uncle Salli was no exception.

I must have been a sight. My shoes had holes in them, and the heel of one shoe was torn away. My short pants had a huge hole that out of embarrassment I covered with my hand so no one would notice. The ship's bathing facilities were nearly nonexistent, so we all were dirty and must have smelled. Well, it didn't matter. We were in America!

Used to years of communal living, we thought that the children's home was to be our new, permanent home. I was soon to find out differently. Uncle Salli got permission to take me to his house for dinner. I was so excited to be in America, I must have babbled the whole way. I was going to see a real American home, and I was going to be with my family. I was in heaven.

But as we walked on Amsterdam Avenue toward his house, Uncle Salli toned down my enthusiasm with a fatherly talk. Among other lessons, he explained two important things. Never walk with your hands in your pockets because this means you are lazy, and never buy a Coca Cola because you would only get a six-ounce drink. Buy Pepsi for a nickel, he said, and you would get double for the same nickel. I have always heeded his advice, and Pepsi is still my drink of choice.

Once again, I was to be disliked by a relative's wife. Uncle Salli's wife, Aunt Rosalia, was not happy to see me. She was under the impression I was going to live with them, and she wanted to set the rules from the start. Fearing that a child would disrupt her home and bring dirt into the house, her first words to me were, "Heinz take off your shoes." But she had nothing to fear because I was not to stay, and after dinner my cousin Martin walked me back to the home.

On the third day, my cousin Milan picked me up, and we went to a men and boys clothing store where he bought me a blue two-piece slack suit and a new pair of shoes. In addition, he bought me another pair of pants and a new shirt. Because they were expensive, he and Norbert split the cost. I didn't care who paid, I just knew I looked and felt great and I loved it. I felt like a grown man in my new long pants. Little boys wore short pants; men wore long pants. I had never had on a pair of long pants before, and the feeling it gave me was heady. Bar mitzvah or no bar mitzvah, it was long pants that really meant I was grown up.

After Sabbath, many of the other kids at the home began leaving for their permanent homes in various cities around the United States. Some went to relatives, others to foster parents and some to orphanages. For the next few days, one by one everyone left. My friend, Fritz, went to Eastown, Delaware to live with his mother and her new husband; my best friend Dudu went to Maryland, N.Y., Josef Moses to New York City, Ernst Valfer and the Kuflik sisters to San Francisco, Elfriede Meyer and Erich Gruenebaum to Chicago, Julius and Siggi Jamner to Brooklyn, Manfred and Evelyn Fuchs to Philadelphia, Anselm Hirsch to Atlanta, Ruth Sanger and Heinz Sinasohn to Los Angeles. I really had no concept of distance because I knew very little about American geography. I just knew they were gone, and I suspected I would never see them again. I had spent so many years with them and had gone through so many happy as well as dangerous times with them, it felt like they were family. I had already been pulled away from my real family. Having to live through that separation pain again with my adopted family was almost more than I could bear.

Finally, Milan came to tell me that I was to go to Shreveport, Louisiana to live with our second cousin, Sam Schuster. I was not very happy about this because I wanted to live with Uncle Moritz Schuster. But Milan convinced the people at the Joint Distribution Committee that I would be better off living with an American family because Uncle Moritz was a very new immigrant himself and would find it difficult enough to find his own way without the burden of a dependant child. And, the Shreveport Schusters were rich. Milan, wanting me to make a good first impression, tutored me to say in English, "Nice to meet you." It was just about the only English I knew.

One afternoon, a counselor at the home asked me to put on my new slack suit and comb my hair. I was now a clean, well-dressed boy of 15. Shortly, they called me into the office where two ladies sat waiting for me. One was diminutive with grey hair; the other was tall, younger and with black hair. They greeted me in English. I answered in English.

"Nice to meet you," I said.

They both laughed and talked to me in English, which was translated by a young man into German. After a few minutes, they smiled and left. The young man informed me that the older lady was from Shreveport visiting the other lady in New York. I had no idea who they were but found out much later that they were relatives who while in New York on other business decided to look me over and see if I was presentable. It was days before I would find out if I was presentable enough.

I was the last child left at the home. Everybody from our transport had gone on to new homes across the country, and I was the only one still there. It was lonely, and it was another two days before my cousin Milan came to tell me that, yes indeed, I was presentable enough and going to Shreveport to live with the Shreveport Schusters.

On the morning of July 10, newlyweds Dr. Robert and Betty Lyons picked me up. Dr. Lyons was a captain in the Army Air Corps., and was stationed at Barksdale Field in Louisiana. I recognized Betty as the younger of the two ladies who had visited me in the home, and I found out she was a Schuster and the daughter of Sam Schuster. The older lady was Uncle Sam Schuster's wife, Perle. I was to live with Uncle Sam and Aunt Perle in Shreveport, Louisiana.

I was amazed when we drove off in the Lyons' beautiful new Chevrolet convertible, a wedding present to each other. What a car! It even had a radio and leather seats! Bob spoke a few words of German that he learned in medical school. Betty had on a very loose-fitting dress and had a rather large belly. During their conversation I heard the word "baby." I finally figured out that Betty was pregnant.

Soon, we arrived at the Lyons' house where I was made to feel at home and was presented with more new clothing: a new shirt and tie. After dinner, Bob played the piano and everyone sang songs I never heard of in a language I didn't understand. In addition to singing, they danced and had a great time. I didn't know what to do or what to expect. Was I supposed to join in on the singing and dancing? Or was I just to sit and be pleasant? For the most part they ignored me. The only being that paid any attention to me was their little Boston bull terrier, Shorty. Shorty looked lonely too, so we kept each other company. Later, when the party died down, they made up a bed for me on the living room couch. I can't remember ever being so glad to call it a day.

The next morning, Bob, Betty, Perle, Shorty and I left by car to go somewhere. They might have told me, but I don't think so. Even if they had, I probably wouldn't have understood. Anyway, Betty, Bob and Perle piled into the front seat, and my newly found friend,

Shorty, climbed in with me in the back. Before we left, they told me to pack my suitcase, a tattered brown leather bag that held all of my meager belongings—belongings that included my new slack suit. I also had a tan leather briefcase that my Uncle Moritz Steinfeld gave me as a bar mitzvah present shortly before I left for France. In the briefcase were my *tallis* (prayer shawl) and my *tefillin* (phylacteries) as well as the *Siddur* that the rabbi in Bois de Boulogne had given me. It wasn't much, but it was all I had left that connected me to my family and my life in Germany. Losing them would be like losing my soul.

At the first stop that evening, Perle, Bob, Betty and I went into a Montgomery Ward department store to buy me pajamas, underpants and undershirts as well as a new toothbrush and toothpaste. We also stopped at a bookstore where Bob bought an English-German dictionary to help us communicate.

That night at dinner, they ordered a steak for me. It was my first nonkosher meal, and I really didn't know what to do. I knew it was wrong to eat this meat, but there was nothing else to eat and no way to tell these Americans the problem. So, I ate it, and it was good.

When nightfall came, we stopped at a tourist-cabin motel. Dr. Lyons and Betty shared one cabin, Perle had another, and I was given a cabin all to myself. I couldn't believe they paid for a private room for me. This was the first time in my life that I occupied a room all by myself, and I didn't like it. I had an incredibly strange feeling. In fact, it was the same feeling I had while living in Burghaun after my visit to Sterbfritz to see my mother. I was 15 years old, but I felt like a little kid, scared and homesick. I cried quietly into my pillow. When, I wondered, would I outgrow this shameful behavior? I was glad to be alone then, happy that no one would find out I cried.

Finally, exhaustion overcame me, and I fell asleep. I slept soundly throughout the night. When daylight came, we met at the establishment's restaurant for breakfast, and Dr. Bob and Betty ordered eggs, toast, a half a grapefruit and milk for me. I had had grapefruit while at the Rothschild Hospital in Paris, so I knew enough to put sugar on the grapefruit to cut the sour taste. Dr. Bob also ordered a half grapefruit on which I saw him sprinkle some while granules from a small container on the table. I figured it was sugar, so I picked up the container and shook a lot of it on my grapefruit—wanting it real sweet. I almost gagged when I took a bite. What I thought was sugar was salt. I had never seen a saltshaker before because salt in Europe was served in an open dish, called a salt celler, along with a tiny spoon. You sprinkled the salt over the food with the spoon. Embarrassed to the gills, I didn't want anyone to know my mistake, and inedible as it was, I ate the whole half grapefruit—salt and all.

The next day, we stopped at a different type of tourist establishment called a motor hotel, and I again had a room to myself. This place was much more luxurious than the first cabin resort we stayed in and had a private bathroom with a shower. The bed was huge, large enough for three people. I never saw anything like it.

In the morning, we breakfasted at a café next to the motor hotel, and this time they didn't order grapefruit. I was never so glad! Back in the car, we headed toward Montgomery, Alabama and after a full day of driving stopped at another motor hotel for the night.

All during this time, Dr. Bob, Betty and Perle spoke very little to me. But that evening at dinner, Dr. Bob brought out the dictionary he bought at the beginning of the trip. He opened it and pointed to the word aunt. He then pointed to Perle and said, "Aunt Perle." From that time on, she was Aunt Perle to me. Why it took them so long to tell me who she was I'll never know.

I don't remember what we had for dinner, but I'll never forget dessert. Dr. Bob ordered ice cream all around and soon the waitress brought four dishes of rose-colored ice cream. I had never seen rose-colored ice cream before. The only ice cream I had ever had was vanilla (cream colored) and chocolate. This ice cream, in addition to being a strange color for ice cream, had little black spots in it, spots I took to be flies. "Well, if in America one eats flies, I also will eat flies," I said to myself. I fast discovered that the dark spots were strawberries. I was greatly relieved. And, it tasted fabulous!

The next morning, I was dressed and ready to go even before Dr. Bob knocked on my door to wake me. When I opened the door, I was surprised to see Bob dressed in a uniform. For the first time, I realized that he was not just Dr. Bob Lyons, but Captain Robert Lyons of the Army Air Corps., and this was the day I would see Maxwell Field, a 20-minute drive from the motel and a place I would call home for a period of time.

At the sentry gate, which just looked like a little house to me, we passed a soldier who saluted—a salute that Captain Lyons returned. We drove to a rather impressive-looking building with a sign that said Officers Club. There, Dr. Bob stopped at the desk and was saluted again. He and the young man spoke for a few minutes while Perle, Betty and I were escorted to a large room with beautiful furniture and a piano. In the corner was an area with lots of bottles and glasses on shelves, a place I was later to find out was a bar. I had never seen or heard of a bar before.

A man dressed with a white jacket greeted us and indicated that we should sit at one of the tables. Again, Dr. Bob ordered for me, and again I ate with relish. I was beginning to really like America. America had great food.

There were so many nice things to look at, and so many good things to eat. And, the music! Looking around, I noticed a music box just like the one at a restaurant we had gone to. I already had been tutored to call this music machine "hootenanny." But, the difference between this music box and the other was that no money was required to play the records. I found songs I liked, and played them. Dr. Bob and Aunt Perle seemed to like them, too. Music often brings people together and it was so with us.

In an adjoining room, a young woman in a white apron stood behind an ice cream bar serving big scoops up in cups or cones. Unlike the music box, the ice cream wasn't free, but I had some money since my Uncle Salli had given me $3 just before I left the home. Seeing me look over the various kinds of ice cream, she asked me what flavor I wanted, and I pointed to a container with cream-colored ice cream. In addition to the flavor, she must have asked me if I wanted it in a cup or a cone. Not knowing what she asked me, I pointed to a stack of cones. For the next two days, I repeated the same routine. I had no idea about American currency, so each time I gave her one of my dollars, she gave me correct change. On the fourth day, I put all the coins on the counter for her to choose the right payment. She must have realized then that I didn't speak English because she laughed while she picked up the proper coins. I don't remember feeling a bit of embarrassment over not knowing English or American currency. The wonderful flavor of the ice cream overcame any discomfort I might have felt about being foreign. And she was so kind, it really didn't matter.

During the day when Dr. Bob was working, I amused myself by swimming in the huge outdoor pool. I wore trunks and had a towel that was supplied by the pool attendant. When I got bored with swimming, I played the jukebox—a song I liked in particular, appropriately turned out to be the Air Corps. song. Many years later, Betty and Bob visited me and my wife, Anita, and while we were reminiscing, Betty told us that I almost drove them crazy playing that song over and over.

The next day while we were eating at a roadhouse near Maxwell Field, Dr. Bob and I tried to converse in his very, very limited German. Midway through the meal, two soldiers with uniforms and

MP armbands came over to Bob who was wearing civilian clothes. They spoke a few minutes, and minutes later everybody laughed. The soldiers then said something to me, patted me on the head and left. I was totally confused and years later Betty explained that the waitress heard us speaking German, thought I was a German spy and called the military police.

I didn't understand a lot of what was going on around me because we couldn't communicate more than just rudimentary things in either German or English. I later learned that while Dr. Bob planned on being at Maxwell Field for only a few days it turned out to be closer to a week. Then plans were change and he was told he would be required to be there for a month.

Because Aunt Perle didn't want to wait a month to get home, it was decided that she and I would continue our journey to Shreveport by train. We piled all our belongings onto the train, a Pullman car. Perle had a compartment and I was given a berth—again luxury beyond belief.

Now, things started to change. Up until then, Dr. Bob and Betty had always been present, and Perle treated me well. But once they were out of the picture, her attitude changed and from that moment on she became, in her own mind, my enemy and treated me with cruelty and abusiveness.

Chapter

TWELVE

The train that carried Aunt Perle and me rolled into Shreveport just after breakfast, and we were greeted by a man who looked just like my father. The man was Sam Schuster, my father's first cousin and Betty's father.

Uncle Sam, a man in his late sixties, was overweight, disheveled and looked as if he needed a shave. He also had no teeth but greeted me with a warm toothless smile and a hug. He immediately dubbed me "Dutchman." The greeting between husband and wife, Bob and Perle, on the other hand, was cold and lacked enthusiasm. I could tell there was no love lost between them.

David Bennet, the black chauffeur, drove up in a two-tone green Buick and loaded our luggage into the trunk. Once everyone was in the car, off we drove to 505 Wilkinson Street. The house was unpretentious, sitting rather high off the street with a narrow driveway that was steep and difficult to maneuver with the car. A professional driver, David easily brought the car up the driveway where he hopped out and started unloading suitcases and bringing them into the house.

Rosalie, the black maid and cook, greeted us warmly as did Julius, Sam and Perle's son. Julius was a short heavy-set 23-year-old man who had Down syndrome. Julius was accompanied by his nurse/companion, Sue, who was also heavyset. I was shocked to see that a relative of mine had Down syndrome, because although I had heard of the condition, no one in Germany ever said anyone in the family had it. No one ever spoke of Julius.

I was familiar with the malady because I had seen it before. A girl in Sterbfritz was also afflicted with the disease, so I didn't feel uncomfortable speaking or interacting with him. I knew how to handle the situation from past experience.

The house was a two-story frame and rather large for its day. On the first floor were two bedrooms, the kitchen, breakfast room, dining room, living room, sunroom and bathroom. The upper floor had two bedrooms, a sitting room and a full bathroom. Sue and Julius shared one of the bedrooms. The second bedroom was Betty's room, empty now and waiting for Betty and Dr. Bob to return. It would be weeks before they would arrive, and their stay would be temporary because Captain Lyons' new orders were to report to the San Francisco Presidio. He would have only a week's layover in Shreveport, but already I was looking forward to their arrival. I knew with their arrival Aunt Perle would treat me better.

The sitting room that was to be my immediate bedroom and had no door, therefore no privacy, a condition that would change once Betty and Dr. Bob left for San Francisco and I was able to move on a permanent basis into Betty's old room.

After showing me around the house, Rosalie prepared lunch, and David, the chauffeur, doubled as a waiter and served it. I was immediately miserable. I spoke no English and no one spoke German or French, the two languages in which I was proficient. What upset me most was that I could feel that there was no love in this family. People seemed only to tolerate one another; open hostility was just under the surface. Everything was formal. Dinner, as always, was in the dining room and served in a formal manner. Sam and Perle exchanged no pleasantries, and I immediately felt that Sue and Julius did not like me and resented my presence as well.

Not only did I feel unwelcome, my own opinion of myself was that I was an oddity. That night after dinner, a line of people traipsed through the front door to meet me, and while everyone was pleasant, I felt like they were looking at me like I was a monkey in a zoo. I wished I was anywhere else but there.

Things started to pick up the next morning when a boy my age came to the house to meet me. His name was Donald, Perle's nephew, more specifically, Perle's sister's son. It didn't take me long to understand that Donald was asking me to go somewhere with him. Where we were going I didn't know, but we walked a short distance to what I realized was a school, Byrd High School. It was June, and the students were on summer break. But on the grounds was a white, wooden building that was the ROTC armory. During the summer, it was used as a recreation hall, and when we entered we met several other kids our age. Everybody knew Donald who explained who I was and why I was there. He must have done a good job because everybody suddenly seemed to be more friendly and sympathetic. Even people in America knew what was going on in Germany, probably more than I knew when I lived there, and because of the language problem definitely more than I knew after I arrived. But everyone seemed to like me, and I felt as if I was accepted as a friend. Things were looking up.

It was an interesting contrast. The people who were not related to me were kinder and treated me better than my own relations. As an adult, I was to learn that many refugees had the same kind of reception from their families. Often, the American relatives were not well off financially, and while they sympathized with the European relatives' circumstances, many viewed the refugee as an interloper—or just another mouth to feed. His or her presence put a financial strain on the entire family.

My circumstance was different. The Schusters were well off, rich even, and they were financially well able to keep me. I eventually came to understand that what I took to be a cool reception from the family was more or less the standard operating procedure for the household. They didn't treat each other any more warmly than they did me. But not having an adult perspective at the time, their lack of affection and caring hurt me deeply.

But the kids accepted me immediately, and there were lots of things to do at the armory. The biggest attraction was Ping-Pong, at least for me. Ping-Pong was my sport; I had played it in France, and I was pretty good at it. Challenged to a game, I played my heart out and beat everyone there, earning their respect. Score one for the refugee! I earned my stripes through Ping-Pong! I played Ping-Pong with the guys every day for a week. Sometimes Donald took me, and sometimes when he was busy, I walked there by myself. I never missed a day, and it was my first real step to becoming an American.

The longer I was in Shreveport, the more I branched out and made friends. By now, I was learning and speaking more and more English every day. Even if I didn't understand the actual words, I could get the gist of what was being said. Another boy my age took me to my first American movie. He was another relative by the name of Louis Lazarus. The movie was "Tom Sawyer," and it was in Technicolor, no less. I didn't understand everything that was said, but I loved it anyway. I loved the color; I loved the action. Technicolor was the best after having only seen movies in black and white.

After the movie, Louis' mother, Bertha, joined us, and the three of us went next door to a drug store where I tasted my first milkshake. It was heavenly. And, Bertha was a wonderful, lovely lady. I liked her immediately. Now I had two new friends: Louis and Donald. And Bertha was like the mother Aunt Perle wasn't.

I had no lack of Shreveport family members and most all of them lived close by as Southern Jews tended to do. Uncle Dave, Sam's brother, lived next door with his wife Leah. Uncle Sam and Uncle Dave were as different as day and night. Where Sam was untidy, Dave was neat as a pin. Uncle Sam's wife, Aunt Perle, was aloof, when not outright hostile. Uncle Dave's wife, Aunt Leah, was always happy and smiling. Aunt Leah was heavy and had a difficult time walking; Aunt Perle was thin and moved quickly. Aunt Perle had children, Aunt Leah had canaries, which she kept in cages in the sunroom where they chirped and sang all day.

I found I had an interesting extended family. Leah's brother, Gus (Happy) Foreman, was a rather unstable man but had been a famous pitcher for the Chicago White Sox. However, he had been involved in the 1919 Black Sox Scandal, that is, players from the White Sox team who were caught fixing the World Series, and was banned from baseball for life. Later, he organized his own ball club in Memphis, Tennessee, calling his team the King David Team. To look the part, all the players were required to grow beards. The team didn't last long, and Happy Foreman moved to Shreveport to be near his sister, where I think Leah more or less supported him.

Leah's nephew, Earl, worked for a produce company as a long-distance driver and drove a semi to California, Texas and even Mexico to pick up produce ordered by the company.

Another of Leah's nephews was a promising Broadway stage actor, but he was killed in a car accident when he a young man.

Then there was Sam's other brother, Mike, who was an entrepreneur. On a trip east, Uncle Mike found a real bargain, a truckload of electric popcorn machines, which he bought at a bargain price. On his way home to Shreveport, he sold all of the popcorn machines in a Pennsylvania town that had no electricity. The man could sell anything to anybody.

What I liked best about Uncle Mike and his wife, Aunt Bess, was their only daughter, Barbara. Barbara was pretty and bright and about my age. We became good friends almost immediately. Barbara was already a high school senior, so she was able to show me the ropes at school. She paved my way in the world of American high school academics.

Another family member was Uncle Dave, another one of Uncle Sam's brothers and a bit of a shyster. The story goes that Uncle Dave owned a blind horse and wanted to sell him. When he found a buyer, he wanted to evade the blindness issue so, he said, "It's a good horse except he doesn't look good. In fact, he don't look at all."

The buyer replied, "What do you mean, it's a pretty horse."

Dave repeated, "The horse don't look good at all."

The horse was sold. The next day, the new owner was furious that Dave had sold him a blind horse. Dave replied, "I told you the horse don't look at all."

I was rapidly learning English, helped along by American movies that I attended almost nightly. Going to the movies was a good way to learn English and it was also a way to stay out of the house and out of Aunt Perle's way. Tickets were only a dime, an expense I could easily afford since Uncle Sam gave me an allowance of $1 a week. That covered both the movie and the popcorn cost. Ah, popcorn. Another American novelty I came to love.

The summer was coming to a close, and the decision had to be made as to what to do with me—enter high school or leave high school and learn a trade. Aunt Perle thought I should become an apprentice to a craftsman. In Jewish families, everybody has an opinion and Aunt Bess Schuster expressed hers loudly. She totally disagreed with Aunt Perle. So much so that she contacted Grover C. Coffman, the Byrd High School principal, to request a conference regarding my future.

During our meeting with Mr. Coffman, it was decided that, in the long run, it would be best for me to start high school in the fall as a freshman. At a subsequent meeting, Mr. Coffman laid out a program of subjects he thought I should take, and on September 4, even though I was a year older than most of the other kids in the freshman class, I started my American high school studies.

I was so happy to have Barbara Schuster walking with me on that first day at Byrd High School. I was so nervous I could say I was actually scared. At the school, Mr. Evans, the assistant principal, escorted me to all my classes, introduced me to my teachers and showed me where my locker was. While I had not missed any classes while I was in the children's home in France, the curriculum here was very different. There was so much to catch up on, but by now my English was good enough that I was able to understand just about everything that was said.

Mrs. Smiley, my English teacher, was a pleasant middle-aged lady who greeted me with a hug. Then, she introduced me to Mrs. Ackerman, the algebra and homeroom teacher, as well as Mrs. McCutchen the history teacher. From there, I was introduced to the football coach who was also to be my gym teacher.

The first order of the new term was issuing books, which the teachers did in each class. Books in Louisiana were free to all students (this was enacted when Huey P. Long was governor). The first day was always easy, and once books were handed out, around eleven o'clock, the students were dismissed.

While I would like to think that the warm reception I got from the teachers was a result of the belief in treating fellow human beings kindly, it was more likely a result of my family's long-standing position in the city. Julius Schuster, my grandfather's brother, came to the United States from Sterbfritz as a 19 year old in 1859. Somehow, he entered the Ohio National Guard almost immediately after arriving in the U.S., and while he didn't have an illustrious military career, upon his discharge he married Barbara Goldschmidt, an American girl born to German immigrants.

Julius and Barbara had 11 children and Uncle Sam was their third child, born in 1873 in Kentucky. For some reason, the family moved from state to state, first going to Omaha and ending up in Chicago.

Young Sam grew up in Chicago and as a young man earned his livelihood as a teamster, mostly because he was smart enough to save his money and buy his own team of horses. He did pretty well for himself, but thinking he could do better elsewhere, in 1913 Sam moved south to Shreveport, Louisiana, and with a meager amount of cash in hand, bought a pushcart and began reselling produce purchased from local farmers. He was so successful with the pushcart that he sold it to buy a wagon. The wagon was bigger and held more produce. He could sell three times as much produce from the wagon as from the pushcart and in the same amount of time. He was so successful, shortly thereafter, he sent for his brother, David, to join him in his new venture.

David, also a smart cookie, had also purchased a horse. Now they had two horses and two wagons. Before long, they were wholesaling the produce to other peddlers and local stores. All this was the beginning of Schuster's Wholesale Produce and Poultry Co. that they located on Water Street. Soon after, brother Mike joined them as well as brother-in-law Ned Lazarus. By 1921, the company had grown into the largest produce company in Northern Louisiana. The company also served east Texas and southern Arkansas. But the time came when the brothers felt ready to branch out even more.

Dave left the produce company and started the Liquor, Wine and Beer Distributing Co., most probably after Prohibition, and both the produce and the liquor companies were highly successful. Eventually, other family members joined them. Young Harold Lazarus ran the day-to-day produce company allowing Sam to venture out into even more endeavors.

By early 1930, Sam Schuster was a very wealthy man. In 1941, when I joined the family, Schuster Wholesale Produce and Poultry Co. had sophisticated freezers, ice-producing equipment, coolers as well as a poultry and egg department. They distributed Maxwell House coffee, shrimp, oysters, packaged butter and a full line of produce. The company had grown into a corporation with a fleet of trucks and a large number of employees.

The produce company was able to finagle lucrative state contracts supplying their products to the state penitentiary in northern Louisiana. It had an equally lucrative contract to purchase crops that were harvested at the prison farm. Cheap convict labor allowed Sam to purchase the produce at lower-than-wholesale prices and then turn a huge profit by selling it at regular retail prices. It was a sweet deal he was able to put together because of his friends in high places. They say it's not what you know but who you know. Uncle Sam knew a lot; but the most important knowledge he possessed was how to influence people in his favor. He played his cards right.

Brother Dave Schuster also knew the right people and just happened to be a personal friend of Governor Huey P. Long, having contributed heavily to Long's political campaign. In addition, the future Louisiana governor, Jimmy Davis, had been a produce company employee and personal friend of the Schuster family prior to entering politics. Davis not only became the governor of the state of Louisiana, he was also a celebrity as a national radio personality with his band. He was also known for having written the wildly popular song "You Are My Sunshine."

The Shreveport Schusters were rich and money just kept pouring in. The Liquor Distributing Co. had the Haig & Haig Scotch, Schenley whiskey and Falstaff beer distributorships plus their own line of wine that was shipped in tank cars from wineries on the West

Coast. Schuster Produce & Poultry Co. was the major produce, poultry and egg supplier for Barksdale Field.

Uncle Sam married Perle Glatstein in 1917. Nepotism abounded. Not only did Sam employ all his own relatives, he also employed members of the Glatstein family. Everything was going smoothly financially and daughter Betty was born in 1918, and son Julius in 1919.

Sam was a rough, uncouth kind of guy who never minced words. He was an equal-opportunity offender and verbally cut loose on most people with whom he came into contact. The flip side of his personality was that he was a very generous man who gave of himself as well as his money. I liked him in spite of all of his bad traits. Though he never said nice things to me, or heaven forbid hugged me, he was generous with his money (probably the only way he knew how to show affection), and I grew to understand and love him over time.

Sam had peculiar sleeping habits. Like clockwork, Sam opened the store at 4 a.m., unlocking the door to let the poultry department manager in so he could feed the chickens. Most of the time, he came home from work at 3 p.m. and slept two to three hours until dinner. After dinner, he went back to bed and got up around 3 a.m., then off to the store at 4 a.m.

He often had trouble sleeping and took Nembutal often. Somehow, he arranged to get the pills from the pharmacist without a doctor's prescription, and on many occasions I went to the drug store to pick up a vial of the pills for him.

As people age, they have a tendency to require several nightly trips to the bathroom. Sam was no exception, but it irritated him that his sleep was interrupted and that he had to get out of bed. That's why he kept a urinal next to his side of the bed. In the morning, Rosalie emptied the urinal, washed it and put it back under the bed.

Not only did he have to urinate frequently, Sam had constant hemorrhoid problems, and his constant use of ointments, like Mentholatum, created a smell that wafted throughout the house, the odor seeping into the wallpaper, upholstery and drapes. I didn't spend much time at home.

After the children were born, Perle and Sam occupied separate bedrooms. Perle was, some said, a total neurotic. I know she stayed in bed most of the day reading dime novels, drinking black coffee and smoking cigarettes. Part of the ill will between Perle and Sam could probably, as strange as it seems, be traced back to the ancient rivalry between German Jews and Eastern European Jews. Sam was a German Jew and Perle came from Eastern European Jewish stock. Aunt Perle may have disliked me because I was another child she had to take care of, or she may have been unhappy to have yet another German Jew in her household. I'll never know.

Whatever her reasons, she made it clear she didn't want me there and certainly did not like me. Like Sam, Aunt Perle minced no words and told me to my face how much she disliked me. I tried to avoid her, tried not to disturb her, but everything I did irritated her. If I tiptoed through the house, she accused me of spying. If I walked normally, I was too noisy. On occasions when she was particularly nasty, Rosalie took me aside and whispered, "You're okay. You're fine." It was encouragement I needed. I loved Rosalie for her kindness, and for a long time she was my only real friend in the house. As much as I appreciated her kindness, there was little Rosalie could do more than say a few encouraging words when I needed them, so I stayed away from the house as much as possible.

Aunt Perle's seat at the dinner table was at the end with my seat to her left. Shortly after I arrived in Shreveport, she instructed me not to sit next to her, loudly proclaiming that I stunk. She may have been right. I wasn't used to the American way of showering every day, nor had I ever used underarm deodorant. She didn't help me out by buying it for me. I had to guess where it might be sold, find it and buy it for myself.

I never ate breakfast at Perle and Sam's because Perle never got up until the afternoon—if she got out of bed at all—and I didn't want to wake her with the clatter of dishes or frying pans. For breakfast, I went to my cousin Barbara Schuster's house where her mother took pity on me and fed me a hearty breakfast every day before school.

Perle's heart never softened toward me even when I needed medical attention. When I caught the flu, I was profoundly ill and was running a very high fever. Instead of taking me to the doctor herself, she told Sue to take me to the hospital because she said she didn't want to have to take care of me. A week later when I was released and came back to the house, she didn't ask how I was but ignored me for a day or two before she started to find fault with me again. The reprieve from criticism was welcome and ended all too soon.

In retrospect, Perle cared for no one but herself. Even her own child, Julius, she came to dislike. When I got back from the hospital, I noticed Perle began keeping away from her Down syndrome son as much as possible and put him totally in Sue's charge. Maybe Julius was the reason Sam and Perle didn't get along. I had the feeling that Sam blamed Perle for Julius' condition, whereas Perle blamed Sam. It was not a happy household, and its problems predated my arrival by many, many years. As a teenager, I was unable to see the big picture, and I felt responsible for the family's unhappiness. I took their problems and placed them squarely on my own shoulders.

Though racism was prevalent in the South, I don't think Sam and Perle ever bought into the racist mentality. For many years, Sam's 1940 Ford coupe was chauffeured by a black man, David Bennett, and Sam treated David well. All in all, the Schusters treated blacks the same way the general white population did, neither good nor bad. I do know that on many occasions Sam would have the chauffeur deliver baskets filled with produce to black families who were in need, and in later years I took over when Sam was no longer able to do so. Sam knew how to make money; he also knew how to spend it to do the most good.

CHAPTER
THIRTEEN

When school started, I could see immediately I was different from the other kids. I not only looked and sounded different, I didn't know what was "hip." In Germany, books were carried in backpacks, a trend that later caught on in the U.S.A. Back then, kids bound books together with a belt and carried them to school that way. I had neither a backpack nor a book belt and stood out, in my own mind anyway, like the proverbial sore thumb.

My nervousness abated, somewhat, when on the first day of school I saw some of the same kids I had played Ping-Pong with. My Ping-Pong chums seemed happy to see me and said hello right away even when all the other kids just stared at me.

About midweek, several of the guys, including a guy named Louis, were talking and laughing so I went up to them and said hello. Greeting me in return, they told me I was just in time to buy some elevator and ice water tickets at a dime each, tickets that, fortunately, they just happened to have on them. I didn't understand why I would need these tickets but figured they must know. So I gave him 20 cents.

They were stifling sniggers while I forked over the money and soon it dawned on me that it was a joke. When I found I had been fooled, I think I laughed harder than anybody, and I remember laughing while looking around to see who I could sell my elevator and ice water tickets to.

Though I thought the joke was funny, maybe a small part of me wanted to get back at Louis, but I didn't consciously consider revenge. But, as luck would have it, I had two classes and gym with Louis. During the first gym class a baseball game was organized. I was so green I had no idea what baseball was. So, they showed me the bat and ball and explained that the point was to hit the ball when it was thrown to me. No further instructions. So, I hit the ball, and I stood there not knowing what to do next. That's when my teammates pointed frantically in the direction of first base and yelled, "Drop the bat and run that way." I got so flustered, I didn't drop the bat, I threw it backwards and it hit Louis in the stomach, knocking the wind out of him. Everything stopped as we watched him gasp for air. I didn't mean to do it, but in retrospect I think it made up for the elevator and ice water tickets gag quite nicely.

My transition from French/German/Jewish culture to American life went fairly easily since the teachers tried to help me as best they could, and the kids were great as well. Mostly, they wanted to know what was really happening in Europe, and I told them as best I could.

Once, the teachers arranged for me to speak in the school assembly. They told me to talk specifically about my experience in getting out of Germany alive. I wasn't sure if this was the best topic for a bunch of kids who knew nothing but a government that guaranteed their freedom, but during the talk, I looked into the audience, and I saw faces that were serious—stony faces. I thought perhaps they didn't understood what I was saying or maybe they didn't like what I was saying. Maybe they didn't like me, or maybe they didn't believe me. I was to find out later that the serious looks were because they were engrossed in what I was saying. When I finished, they gave me a standing ovation—something I didn't understand at the time. But they were clapping their hands for me so I figured they must have liked my talk.

About this time, I was introduced to American sports other than baseball. I was rather stocky for my height, and some of the guys told me I'd be good at football—a sport I knew as much about as baseball. But I was willing to learn, and on the first day of practice they put me in a uniform. It was huge, and I felt like the Pillsbury dough boy with all the padding and a helmet that blocked my vision and wobbled on my head. It was hot, but the coach made us run laps anyway. Sweating from the heat and the heavy uniform, I thought I would die right out there in the field. But I didn't, and it was then I decided that American football was not for me.

As a sophomore, I began to feel a strong sense of patriotism for the country that befriended me, so I was happy to join ROTC. Well, I was required to take an extracurricular class, and it beat gym. So, ROTC it was.

The first ROTC class was a disaster. Though it seems a simple enough task, I didn't know how to march and had to be taught. In Germany, all marching was done with a "goose step." In America, the march was much different. So, when I goose stepped a few yards, I had them doubled over with laughter. Later, they calmed down enough to teach me the right way to march.

I liked the ROTC uniform well enough because first, it looked good, and second it was a lot lighter than the football uniform, though not by much. The big problem was that it was made from my old nemesis—wool. As far back as I can remember, I hated itchy wool touching my skin, and the ROTC uniforms were made of 100 percent wool. To keep me from scratching my skin raw, as I was sure would happen if I had to wear the uniform all day long, I wore my pajama bottoms beneath the pants—like long underwear. That did the trick, but I was heavy enough without the extra padding. I must have looked like a fat German sausage with the long johns.

I loved going to school in America. It was such a contrast to my school life in Germany. When the Nazis enforced their anti-Semitic policies and Lehrer Weidling became abusive, understandably I was not motivated to do schoolwork and my grades suffered. My scholastic performance was so bad in the German school that Weidling held me back a year, yet another humiliation that made me hate going to school.

But in America, it was different. Teachers helped me, didn't humiliate me and often stayed with me after class to tutor me. Sometimes they invited me to their homes for dinner with their families. For the first time since my early childhood, I felt wanted and special. I needed this kindness and help because the school work was hard enough all by itself; it was even harder to do the lessons in a language I was just learning. But with all the help I got, I did extremely well and was able to earn good grades in my first year in the Shreveport high school.

Language-wise, I had it all over the American kids who spoke only English. By my second year, my English was pretty good, and in addition I was fluent in French and German. My first book report was on a book written in French. I borrowed it from Mme. Blanc, the French teacher, who allowed me to read it and give my report on it—in French and in English, something that made me a huge novelty with the kids. Some thought I was really cool, and they wanted to be my friends. Probably others didn't think I was all that hot, but they never said anything.

Also in my second year, I took a civics class and I was spellbound. I had never heard of the concept of equality. I was incredulous that the laws of America actually secured an individual's right to life, liberty and the pursuit of happiness—unheard-of concepts in a dictatorship like Germany. Having individual rights was almost beyond my comprehension. In retrospect, if a concept like individual rights had been a part of German culture, perhaps the travesty against what Hitler called "undesirables" would not have happened.

I was quickly becoming Americanized and was learning all the American customs. The best of times was around Christmas when I was invited to a party and learned that if you stood under the mistletoe, a girl would come and kiss you. We also played spin-the-bottle—another game I looked forward to. I especially loved the kissing games when Bettina Hillman kissed me. Bettina was a very pretty 14-year-old girl who was not only a delight to look at but bright scholastically as well as a talented musician. I fell in love—again. It seemed I was always falling hopelessly in love with pretty women.

American high school was different from any other school experience I had ever had. For the first time I was on my own. No one ever asked me, "Did you do your homework?" But I managed to do well and with an hour of study hall and sitting in the sitting room for about an hour I had no problem completing my daily homework.

My life was totally different from my German or French life. From the first day in New York City, I didn't live a Jewish life. It upset me at first that my Shreveport family didn't observe Jewish customs, and in fact acted more like a Christian family. On Christmas, a cut evergreen tree was dragged into the house, set in a metal stand, and ornaments of all kinds and descriptions were placed on it. A round red skirt hid the tree stand, and colorful packages done up in ribbons and bows were placed under the tree. The gifts were to be exchanged with other family members on Christmas Eve. I was Jewish and uncomfortable with all of it; this was totally against all my beliefs, but I had no choice and had to participate. I was beholden to these people, so I had no right to criticize.

But, I had expected something different since both Sam and Perle came from observant families. Perle's parents, who lived in Shreveport, kept a kosher home and observed religious laws and customs. No Christmas tree ever entered their house, and I can only believe the Sam Schuster household's Christmas celebration caused them to heave a heavy sigh.

But Uncle Sam made up for the lack of Jewish observance. On my first Rosh Hashanah in Shreveport, he took me to the evening service at the local Reform temple, a gesture I'm certain he did for my benefit alone, because while he was a paying member of the congregation, this was the only time I can remember him attending a temple service.

But while Sam didn't observe Jewish laws, he catered to those who did. I remember on Thursdays a *shochet* (ritual slaughterer) would come to Schuster's Poultry and perform the ritual slaughter of chickens for the only kosher meat market in town. Even if he himself didn't adhere to the Jewish dietary laws, he made sure those who wished to do so could.

The most pleasant memories of my life in Shreveport were the times I spent at the riding academy, a place my Uncle Sam bought when the owners fell into hard times and needed quick cash. They sold the horses, barns and land to my uncle, and as luck would have it, it not only prospered as a riding stable but in later years there was an oil strike on the property. Everything Uncle Sam touched turned to gold, in this case black gold, and he was getting richer by the day.

But, when I first started going to the stables, Sam Schuster's only connection was that he boarded two horses there. Irene, the owner, lived with her family in one of the dilapidated houses in the back. There were also three black men who were the grooms and stable hands, and one of them was old man Clem, a guy who could hardly walk. The other man, named Shorty, was not more than four feet tall, and Buster, who was young and the only one who had any education.

I remember Shorty lived in the tack room with a woman, something that was common in those days. One Sunday when Sam and I arrived at the academy, Buster ran out to our car. Breathless, he told us that Shorty had just died while feeding the horses. His body was still lying in one of the stalls. Not knowing what to do, the woman he lived with was almost in hysterics. So Sam called his friend, Judge Underwood, and asked him what to do with Shorty's corpse. The judge told him not to worry, that he would take care of it. Within the hour, the coroner arrived accompanied by two men from the morgue. It wasn't hard to lift Shorty's slight body into the truck and take it away. While it took a few days for the excitement to wear off, normalcy did return, and it wasn't long before Clem moved into the tack room with Shorty's woman.

In Shreveport, life went on and the ties to my past were disintegrating. I was now a typical young American boy who went to high school, joined Boy Scouts, played Ping-Pong, dated girls and looked forward to entering the military to help free Europe. Those who were old enough were signing up right and left. The kids who were too young to sign up for the military occupied themselves with thoughts of learning how to drive a car—just as they do today. I was one of those kids.

In Louisiana at that time, driver's licenses weren't required, and it didn't take long before I was able to con people into teaching me how to drive. Once I was able to prove my driving proficiency to my uncle, he let me be his Sunday chauffeur.

Every Sunday, Sam came upstairs to my room at 7 a.m. and woke me. Then, we'd hop into the Buick and drive to the Washington Uhry Hotel for breakfast. When we finished eating, we went to the store. Then, around 10 a.m., Harold called the weekly sales meeting to order. Uncle Sam always attended the sales meetings thinking it was an important gesture that would encourage the salesmen to work harder. He sincerely liked them all, always greeting each one by name. Never staying more than an hour, we'd then jump back into the Buick and drive around to visit his old customers. Often more than one customer asked us to join them for lunch. Not wanting to offend anyone, we always stayed and ate with feigned relish. Some days, we had so many lunches I thought we would pop.

Around noon, we'd go to the stables for an inspection tour. It was about that time that Sam purchased a new horse named Kaiser. Now, Kaiser had not been tested to see how he would react to a new rider, and I, eager to try him out, threw a Western saddle on him and jumped on his back. Before one of the grooms had a chance to close the gate to the ring, Kaiser took off at a full gallop. I had no control over the horse. Pulling back on the reins as hard as I could had no affect. He galloped down the dirt road, then veered off through the backyard of a house. I leaned forward across his neck as tight as I could, my head just missing the wire clotheslines that could have decapitated me.

I was so scared, I knew I had to get off, but the horse wouldn't stop. Finally, I slipped my feet out of the stirrups and made myself slide off the saddle onto the ground, making sure I would fall out of the way of the horse's hooves. I rolled a few times, and luckily, didn't bang my head on anything more solid than turf. Kaiser, feeling the freedom of riderlessness, came to a halt in a nearby backyard and eyed my prostrate form with self-satisfaction. A little bruised, I scrambled to my feet and brushed off the dirt. I had just been outsmarted by a horse, but I didn't care. I was just glad to be alive. Kaiser, tired of the game he had won so easily, allowed me to gather up his reins and walk him back to the stables.

After giving myself a little time to recover, I drove Sam to the Harmony Club for his Sunday poker game, which gave me the use of the Buick for the rest of the afternoon. The times I was given the car all to myself, my friend, David Nevin, waited on his front porch for me to pick him up. I started honking the horn halfway down the street, a signal that meant he was to run to the curb to meet me. When I pulled up, he would hop into the passenger seat with one clean motion. Gunning the engine, our weekly joyride would begin. I can still remember the carefree feeling we had. The cool wind in our hair and faces, the sun shining warmly through the windows. We thought nothing could spoil it for us.

On December 7, 1941, Japan attacked Pearl Harbor in Hawaii and the United States quickly declared war on Japan. Canada followed suit in a matter of days. On December 11, 1941, Germany declared war on the United States.

But something did spoil it. On Sunday, December 7, 1941, Dave Schuster barreled through the kitchen door and told us that the Japanese had attacked Pearl Harbor. I had no idea what or where Pearl Harbor was, but it sounded serious. Over lunch, we talked about the attack with as much information as we had.

"We'll declare war on Japan and Germany," Dave said, adding, "We'll beat those bastard Germans and Japs in less than six months."

"I don't believe it," I countered. "I don't know about Japan, but I saw Germany's army. And I saw the fanaticism of the Nazis. They'll be hard, if not impossible, to beat."

"What? Are you a Nazi?" he asked, looking at me in disbelief.

"No," I virtually screamed at him. "But you haven't seen what I've seen," I yelled, running from the table to keep myself from taking a punch at him. Julius, thinking it was funny, screamed the word Nazi at my retreating back. All he knew about Nazis was what singer Kate Smith, of all people, said about them on her radio program. She said they were from Germany so in Julius' mind, anyone from Germany must be a Nazi. Julius' world revolved around radio shows. If it wasn't Kate Smith, it was Eddie Cantor or Fanny Brice's Baby Snooks. He didn't know what I knew because he hadn't seen what I had seen or been through what I had been through. So many American Jews, especially the kids, were so ignorant about what was happening in the rest of the world. Maybe that was a good thing.

I still remembered the harsh treatment I had gotten from the Nazis, but with all the diversions American life provided, it often seemed like a bad dream. I still heard from my mother and sisters occasionally. If they were being mistreated, they didn't tell me. Maybe they were, but they didn't want me to worry, and I didn't. Talk of war took a back seat and life returned to normal.

Sam Schuster wanted me to become more Americanized and what was more American than Boy Scouts? One of my friends, David Nevin, was a Boy Scout and Sam asked his mother if David would invite me to his next Boy Scout troop meeting. I was thrilled to be asked, and after attending a meeting I joined right away.

The Boy Scout troop held meetings in a small building behind a church. The building was big enough, but it only had one open room, and with a number of different squads it needed to be remodeled with individual areas for submeetings. The scout master asked if anyone knew how to do woodworking. I was again happy that my experience as a woodworker could be put to good use for my new friends, and I was immediately put in charge of building the compartments, a job I went about completing happily.

I looked up to David for good reason. He was the guy I wanted to be—smart, good looking, and a guy who got things done. David was the American I wanted to be. Shortly after my Scout initiation, David passed all the requirements to become an Eagle Scout, which made him even more important in my eyes. David and I became inseparable, and his friends became my friends.

Our circle now included two more guys: Howard Kidder and Jack Shelton. Jack's father was the manager of the local YMCA, where we swam in the indoor pool. I was happy and my friendships were growing. I now had David, Howard and Jack as friends, as well as Donald and Louis. My world was expanding.

In addition to friends, boys need spending money, and since my aunt and uncle were not disposed to doling money out for nothing, I first got a job as a paperboy and later advanced to a better-paying job as a bag boy at the Big Chain grocery store close to the house. My pay was 25 cents an hour plus tips. As a bag boy, we carried groceries to the customers' cars. Most of the time, we got great tips, sometimes as much as a nickel—big money in those days.

In December of 1941, Bob and Betty Lyons became first-time parents with the birth of their son, Michael, and Aunt Perle flew from Shreveport to San Francisco to be with Betty and help with the new baby. It was a huge experience for the whole family. Babies were born every day, but flying to somewhere so far away was not an everyday occurrence. Aunt Perle's flight was more of a wonderment than the ordinary occurrence of a child's birth.

Then, in March of 1942, Bob was transferred to the newly organized 8th Air Force that was based in England where he was to be the senior flight surgeon. It was decided that Betty and baby Michael should return to Shreveport in Bob's absence, and with the help of Sue, who further added to the family excitement by also flying to San Francisco, helped Betty drive back to Shreveport in a newly acquired 1941 Buick.

True to form, after Betty's return, my life with Aunt Perle improved somewhat. Betty was my friend and my advocate, and when finally Sue realized that I was no threat to her status in the family, she became my friend as well. With Sue conquered, Julius also became my friend. My home life was improving, too.

Looking back, I recognize that I was what is now called "a survivor." I survived because I was able to close myself off emotionally from all the hurt and bad things that happened to me and around me. I was devastated at first to leave my mother and sister and the life I knew in Germany, but I also knew I had to struggle through, if not for myself, then for them. I always tried to make the best of every situation, though the situations were often horrendous.

It's hard enough for adults when they think someone dislikes them. For children, it's worse than hard because children have no power. But from infancy my mother, father and sisters had given me a solid emotional base. I had been loved by my mother and father and doted on by my sisters. I knew I was loveable even when others like Lehrer Weidling hated me, and when Aunt Erna took such an immediate dislike to me. I was even able to shrug off Aunt Perle's cruel treatment. I was who I was, and that was that. I closed it off and went about my business. I had two separate lives: my fun, kid life and the more sobering life at home with Aunt Perle. But, I knew I would get through it and I did.

It was hard to ignore the war now because the entire country was patriotic and united behind the war effort. War bond drives were organized everywhere, and people saved everything—tin foil, used metals, suet and anything that could be reused for the war effort. Rationing was in full force with items that included gasoline, coffee, meat and cigarettes.

Among other patriotic acts, Byrd High School students organized a used-metal drive. I remember scrounging the neighborhood for as much scrap metal as I could find as did the other students. I don't think I found very much though I looked everywhere. But the combined effort of all the kids culminated in a huge pile of scrap metal, which we delivered to and piled high in the school's front yard. It made a scrap-metal mountain that we proudly knew would single-handedly win the war.

Everyone was in a party mood and sometime during the early afternoon an announcement came over the P.A. system that declared Louis Lazarus and Henry Schuster the school's champion scrap-metal collectors. Neither Louis nor I had any idea why we had been chosen since others seemed to bring in as much scrap metal as we did. But one of the items that Louis' family brought over later was a heavy old truck scale from my family's business, one that had recently been replaced by a newer model. The scale sat high atop the metal mountain, gleaming in all its scrap-metal glory. What tipped the scale in our favor was the truck scale.

Now, with the newspapers filled daily with news from the front, everyone wanted to know what was going on in the war and what it was like in Germany. The principal, Mr. Coffman, was a member of the local Kiwanis Club, and he arranged for me to speak to the group about my experiences as a Jewish boy living in Nazi Germany. I had a lot to tell, most of it bad. Yet, even I didn't know the worst of it. While there were rumors, until the American soldiers liberated the concentration camps, the rumors were just that—rumors.

At first, I was frightened to speak before so many strangers, but I soon overcame it when I said a couple of things that made them laugh. What they thought was funny was what Germans thought of Americans.

"The Americans are crazy," I said to a quiet audience. "First, they boil water to make tea, and then they add ice to make it cold. They add sugar to make it sweet, and then they squeeze in lemon to make it sour! What could be crazier than that?"

I got a big laugh, and I knew then that if you were funny, people would like you. Being liked was so important to me then because in

Nazi Germany it seemed no one liked me. Even if I was funny in Germany no one would have liked me because I was Jewish. Being Jewish wasn't a drawback in America, and it wasn't long before I was invited to speak at other organizations and churches. Everybody, it seemed, wanted to know what it was like for Jews in Germany.

Shortly after the war broke out, gas rationing prohibited the Schuster Produce Co. and the liquor company from making second daily deliveries to their customers. Ever the schemer, Sam resolved the problem. A horse and wagon from his riding academy would come to the store and make the second day's deliveries to accommodate their customers.

Dixie Girl (originally Julius' horse) was the horse designate. Buster, from the academy, became the deliveryman. On occasions when a truck driver didn't show up, Buster drove one of the delivery trucks in the morning and made the additional deliveries by horse and wagon in the afternoon.

By then, Dixie Girl was old, and Sam decided that it would be smart to have a backup horse, and one ought to be broken in. I was good with horses, having been around them all my life, and I volunteered to do the job. Dixie Dan, Dixie Girl's foal, was the best-suited candidate, and every day after school I went to the stable and worked him. It didn't take long before he was ready to be hitched to a wagon, and Dixie Dan became every bit as good a wagon horse as his mother Dixie Girl.

If life with Aunt Perle was unpleasant, life with Sam Schuster was equally as pleasant. Something was always going on. On days when Sam didn't fall asleep directly after dinner, we went to watch the Shreveport Sports, a class A minor league team, play baseball. On other occasions, we stopped by a local bowling alley to watch the Schuster Womens' Bowling Team. Sometime in 1943, Sam invited

David Nevin and me to a cockfight. It was against the law, but since the local sheriff was in attendance, we didn't fear arrest. David and I would bet (maybe a nickel) on each fight, and I was able to pick the winning rooster every time.

In retrospect, cockfighting is a pretty gruesome sport, however it took years and lots of exposure to other ways of thinking to make me see how awful it really was. The cruelty of cockfighting and dog fighting has been in the news of late, and it is, indeed, a cruel sport and one that I'm glad is outlawed. On the other hand, we also went to professional wrestling matches, which at times were as bloody as the cockfights. The only difference is that the wrestlers have a choice; the animals do not.

It was about that time we got into raising rabbits. The beginning of our rabbit farm came as a result of Dave Schuster attending a war bond rally sometime in March, at which various items were put up for auction. At one of the auctions, Dave bought a female white rabbit and brought it to the house as a present for baby Michael. We let the cute little creature hop around the house for a while, leaving her signature pellets everywhere she went. But once the novelty wore off, we realized we had no place to keep her.

Sam suggested that I take her to the horse academy. Instead, David and I decided this would be a perfect time to get involved with the 4-H Club. Mary Nevin agreed to let us keep the bunny in their backyard, and in a day or two Sam had a wire chicken coop delivered. We now had the proper beginning of our rabbit farm.

Somehow, we found out that a fireman at the local fire station was raising white pedigreed rabbits, so we decided to visit the station to ask what the best way was to start our enterprise. When we told him how we got the rabbit, he laughed and said that the rabbit had been his and was one he had donated for the auction. Not only did he give us the rabbit's pedigree papers, he also gave us a male white rabbit, also with the proper papers. We were legit!

Within six months, our two, sweet little white rabbits were 30 sweet little white rabbits. Some of the males we traded with the fireman for more breeding females. We had hundreds of rabbits, and it was so time consuming it began to interfere with my schoolwork. I was no longer an A student and neither was David. School and a proper education came first in the Schuster family, as in almost all American Jewish families, and consequently, we were encouraged, if not told outright, to give up the rabbit business. Since we were yet to realize any financial gain from the endeavor it made sense to close it down, which we did.

Unfortunately, however, not before some of our rabbits came down with the dangerous rabbit fever, an illness caused by bacterium Francisella tularensis, and one that can be passed to humans through contact with infected tissues or ticks. So that the disease wouldn't spread, our fireman friend took over and disposed of all our rabbits. It was a sad day for David and me. Sadder for the rabbits.

In one of the back pages of a May 1942 issue of The New York Times, it was reported that the Nazis had killed over 100,000 Jews in the Baltic countries of Latvia, Lithuania, and Estonia. The same number of Jews were killed in Poland, and 200,000 Jews were killed in Russia.

When school let out for the summer in 1942, I got a job at the Schuster Liquor, Beer and Wine Distributing Co. where I worked side-by-side with two black men washing bottles that had been returned from various retail stores. Due to the glass shortage, all bottles had to be recycled.

These two guys were not the first black men I had ever seen. There was a black man at the stables and a black man had been Sam's chauffeur. As a little boy, I remember seeing an American black man in Sterbfritz. His job was to travel through the German towns selling Aunt Jemima pancake syrup. But these guys were very different from the other blacks I had known. It was my contact with these blacks that gave me a real education about life and language that I had never before been exposed to. I knew about the facts of life but never in such graphic detail as came out of their mouths; they explicitly described their bedroom (and elsewhere) accomplishments and how the ladies just begged them for it. Every other word was the "F" word, a word I had heard spoken before but not with quite such relish, or with as many syllables.

I was very interested in girls myself and I had a girlfriend then, the lovely Bettina Hillman whom everyone called Tina. Tina, in addition to being extremely pretty, was a straight-A student. I was so smitten by the lovely Tina that I made excuses to go to her house and see her. When I ran out of excuses to knock on her door, my friend David Nevin and I devised a plan to make her come out to us.

We knew if she thought I was hurt she would run to my aid, so I practiced falling off my bicycle along with limping with a feigned sprained ankle. I had my act down pretty good and quickly took my bicycle-riding routine over to Bettina's house. Making a couple of practice passes in front of her house to get her attention, my third pass culminated in my pretend fall. It worked! The lovely Tina flew from her house to my side. With cool hands she felt my fevered brow as well as my legitimately swollen ankle and helped me into her house. I spent the rest of the afternoon with the beautiful Bettina, but it was a high price to pay for love.

Bettina was later to become Dr. Bettina Hillman, well-known physician. Perhaps the bicycle incident was the impetus for her career choice. I'll never know, but I will always be proud to have been her first patient.

As a sophomore, I had classes in English, civics, a course called nations at work where I learned about other countries in the world, algebra, ancient history and debate. I also joined the drama club. On many Friday evenings, the drama club performed one-hour programs over the local radio station KRMD. I always had the Yankee parts because I spoke the best "Northern English." Before the advent of television, most everyone in the South spoke with a Southern accent, but I learned to speak English with only a slight Southern drawl. Perle and Sam both were originally from the North, and my association with them and the Nevin family influenced my English for the better.

Dogs have always been a huge part of Southern life. Mostly outdoor creatures, nearly every family had at least one dog. The Nevin's dog, Juneau, was a very gentle American pit bull female who had a litter of pups prior to being spayed. I don't know how many puppies were in the litter, but two, Lightning, a white male, was given to Bob Lyons. Another in the litter was Champion, also a white, who went to other relatives. Lightning was trained to be a fighter and was vicious and dangerous. Champ was exactly the opposite, a lovable and gentle dog who roamed the neighborhood and very often, followed me to school.

When Betty and Bob left for California, Lightning had to stay behind and was chained to a doghouse at the Broadmore Stables. It was almost impossible to come near him, and his food had to be thrown to him and water was supplied with a hose from a distance. Because he was so dangerous, Sam had the dog pound pick him up where he was kept in an enclosure by himself. For a dollar, we would often buy twenty hamburgers from a hamburger stand around the corner and feed them to him through the chain link fence.

While Juneau really belonged to David, she didn't know if she was David's dog or my dog because I always paid so much attention to her. She would often follow either David or me to school, and once when she couldn't find me she tracked me down and found me in the classroom. Everybody thought it was funny to have a dog in school. I thought it was great because I got out of class to take Juneau home.

There were times when I was really happy Juneau liked me. Sometimes, I took my bike to the academy directly from school and once on the way a chow chow dog ran after me. I thought the dog was dangerous, and it scared me. The next day, I had Juneau follow me and when the chow ran up, it saw Juneau who took off after it. On another occasion, as I was passing the chow's house, he again came after me. I made believe that Juneau was with me, yelling for her and calling her name. Hearing Juneau's name, the chow tucked his tail between his legs and ran away. Juneau saved me even when she wasn't there.

In addition to school work, I was always busy with a job of some sort. In the autumn of 1942, I went back to work as a bag boy at the Big Chain store. When the produce manager was drafted, and because my family was in the produce business, they thought I knew all about produce so they made me the part-time produce manager, a job I liked. I felt like a big shot being made produce manager at the age of 16.

Along with some of the quick-sale produce, I was allowed to take home day-old cookies, cakes and bread from the store, something I was proud to do because it felt like I was paying back, even in such a small way, the family that had taken me in and given me a home. It felt good to be able to help out though Aunt Perle never acknowledged my contributions, nor did she ever thank me. I don't think I expected it from her, but a thank you would have been nice to hear.

Then there was the job at the ice company. Again, they were short drivers because of the draft. I was a pretty husky kid, so I was hired on as a driver's helper. More "life education" came from this driver, who was a raunchy character, and his girlfriend, a pretty young woman who was a hooker. The driver thought David and I should learn about the facts of life, so he arranged for us to lose our virginity with his hooker girlfriend. (We did, but, not at the same time.)

One morning, the driver didn't show up for work and the dispatcher yelled, "Schuster, do you know how to drive a truck?" I had never driven the truck before, but I knew how to drive a car so I said, "Yes!" For the rest of the summer I was an iceman driving an ice truck and making pretty good money.

It was in 1942 that I heard from my mother and sisters for the last time. For a while, I thought they were just too busy to write, but soon rumors came out of Germany that not only the men were being placed in concentration camps but the women also. I feared for them but was powerless to do anything. If I thought about it too much I think I would have gone crazy. So I occupied myself with the things typical American kids do to keep busy.

School was still my top priority, and in my last year at school I decided to take six subjects and finish up because I knew that after my 18th birthday I would be eligible for the draft. I was anxious to join up. I wanted to do what I could to conquer Germany even if it was my homeland. My homeland had turned against me and my family, and I felt no loyalty to it.

To graduate early, with only three years of high school, I was allowed to take a French exam for extra credit. German was not offered by Byrd High School but I passed a German proficiency test at Centenary College for credit as well. The only subject that posed a problem was chemistry. I didn't like it and wasn't good at it, but I was able to earn a good grade from the teacher by doing "extra-credit" work at his sheep farm.

The chemistry teacher, Mr. Diener, had a small sheep farm approximately a mile from the Broadmore Stables. A couple of times I rode one of the horses to his place to pay him a visit. In the spring, he sheared the sheep with a manual clipper, a really laborious endeavor. To make things easier for him, I borrowed the electric clippers we had at the academy, and using them we sheered the wool in less than half the time. I was now one of Diener's favorite students, and though my grasp of chemistry wasn't any better than before, our friendship helped me through the course. To better my grade, Diener asked me to write a report in addition to the test. I said I would, but I "borrowed" my paper from Donald Zadek, who wrote his paper the prior school year and had gotten a good grade for it. I don't know if Mr. Diener recognized the paper. If he did, he didn't say anything, and he gave me a B. With gratitude, I took it without question.

In 1942, towards the end of the summer school break, it was suggested that relatives should take me with them to Bloomington to visit my Uncle Moritz and Aunt Toni Schuster, whom I had not seen since I arrived in the United States. The plan was presented to Perle who got furious and went into a temper tantrum. Screaming, "No way will he go," she stamped her foot. Our relationship had improved since Betty had returned, so her outburst surprised me. Plead as I might, she wouldn't change her mind, and Sam just wanted to keep the peace and didn't push it. I never found out why she wouldn't let me go. But her unreasonableness increased the division between us.

I had built up hope of seeing Uncle Moritz and the thought of not being able to do so depressed me. True to form, I walled myself off against the pain, and I soon jollied myself out of it by going to an Abbott and Costello movie and laughing myself silly. I would not allow Aunt Perle or anyone else to get to me.

During Christmas vacation, Sam's niece, Goldie, her husband and 23-year-old son, Ned, came for a visit from New York City so

I had to give up my room for Goldie and her husband. Every time someone visited, I had to give up my room and this was just one more time. Ned and I made up a bed for ourselves in the room above the garage. He seemed a little odd to me, but I couldn't pinpoint why. Maybe that was how New Yorkers were. But that night, I was to find my perceptions were right on target when he made sexual advances. Recalling the incident years earlier at the Waisenhaus, I not only rejected his advances, I punched him— hard! Apparently undaunted, he tried again sometime later—while I was sleeping. I woke up and shoved him out of bed. Then I threw his pillow and a blanket at him and told him to sleep on the floor, which he did. I didn't have any more trouble with him for the rest of the visit.

FOURTEEN

Jews in Nazi Germany were desperate to leave, and several of my relatives tried all means possible to get out. If they were not able to get to the United States, they tried to get to China, Cuba and the Dominican Republic. But everyone hoped to find an American sponsor who would supply affidavits of support. Many of my family members wrote to Sam asking him for help, and he agreed to supply anyone from the family with a guarantee of support, which ended up being approximately 15 Schuster families in addition to several more who no longer had the Schuster name. Fortunately, Sam was well off, and he was allowed to supply affidavits for as many as he could afford. Others, those who couldn't get sponsors, were not so lucky.

My desire to fight the Germans was realized on March 18, 1944, my 18th birthday, when I registered for the draft, and on May 20 I boarded a bus taking new enlistees to Camp Beauregard near Alexandria, Louisiana. We arrived late in the evening and found that no one was expecting a busload of inductees. It was close to midnight and everyone was sleeping so it took some time to find someone who was awake, let alone someone who could find us a place to sleep. We hadn't eaten since noon, so someone rustled up boxes of K rations for dinner, my first experience with fine military cuisine.

The next morning the brass finally realized why we were there and induction began with physicals. Ordered to strip naked, we were issued a small, cloth drawstring bag for our valuables, which we were told to tie around our bodies. Doctors gave physical exams in small semiprivate cubicles.

By that time, I spoke English well and was accent free; however I didn't know all the American idioms. I was instructed to move down the line to the third cubicle where the doctor told me to bend over and spread my cheeks. You guessed it. I bent over and put my hands on my face and spread my cheeks. The doctor laughed so hard he almost collapsed. When he could compose himself, he called the other doctors into the cubicle and asked me to repeat my performance. I was the laughing stock.

After physicals, everyone, except me, was given khaki and woolen uniforms in olive drab. Included in the package were underpants, undershirts, razors, toothbrushes and army boots. All I got was a helmet liner and the boots. Because I was not yet a citizen and my nationality was German, no one knew what to do with me. For the next week, I was the only soldier dressed in civilian clothes, a helmet liner and boots. But they gave me dog tags (identification tags) with my full name, blood type and religion. My tag had a big H on it for Hebrew.

Last of all, I was given an IQ test at which I did fairly well, but I was sure I could do better, so in about three months when the test would be given again, I asked to be retested. This time, I did extremely well. I just needed practice.

It was about this time I told my commanding officers that I wanted to be in the air corps. I felt I had never had another nationality but American, and I was anxious to fight Germans. Flying fighter aircraft seemed like the best way to do that, but I was told that because I wasn't a citizen, for me the air corps. was out. Only American citizens were allowed to fly military planes. I was not pleased with the rule, but I was lucky to be allowed in the Army Air Corps. and was happy with that.

Not only was Camp Beauregard an induction center for the United States southern district, it was also an encampment for German prisoners of war. The language problem made communication, or interrogation, impossible. When the base commander found out I spoke German, I was pressed into service as an interpreter, a job that kept me occupied for the remainder of my stay at the camp.

When I arrived at the POW camp, I spoke only English to the other Americans so the German POWs assumed I didn't know German. They were a nasty bunch, slinging racial epithets at their jailers and me not knowing I understood. When they learned I spoke German, they sneered that I must be a damn Jew. They were as ugly as they could be since they knew the Geneva Conference rules and regulations pertaining to prisoners of war would protect them. There was nothing we could do to them, and they knew it.

In addition to German interpreting, I was asked to interpret French as well. Several Louisiana Cajun inductees spoke no English, and I was asked to accompany them through their physical exams and translate instructions to them as well as their verbal responses. But the French they spoke was Cajun French, and I didn't understand a word they said. I don't think they understood me either. I wasn't much help so they sent me back to the Germans.

Shortly after, I got approval from headquarters, and I was placed on a transport to Shepherd Field, Texas for basic training. There, I was assigned to Company C, Platoon 4. Our drill instructor was a corporal and a mean guy who had been a New York City cop before he enlisted. He thrived on picking on me and the two other Jewish soldiers at the barracks. Looking at my dog tags that clearly had the letter "H" for Hebrew, thereafter he referred to me as "Jew Boy." He made life as unpleasant as he could during our time there. I almost felt as if I had been transported back to Lehrer Weidling's class. Anti-Semitism was not exclusively a German aberration.

Approximately two or three days after our arrival, our company and several others marched to the base assembly hall for an indoctrination briefing. There, we were welcomed by the base commander, a brigadier general, chaplains for the various faiths and several doctors. The physicians' topic was general health with an emphasis on venereal disease. He explained the use of condoms and especially the "pro stations" in most cities. (A pro station stands for prophylactic station. The so-called station was identified with a green light above the door.) The first thing he did was to explode the myth that you could get infected from a toilet seat. He said the only way you could get a venereal disease from a toilet seat was if you took the woman into the toilet with you.

Our Jewish chaplain, Major Goldstein, invited all the Jewish personnel to meet with him after the conclusion of the briefing. My guess is there were 20 to 30 soldiers with the letter H on their dog tags. I was the only one from the South, and I was immediately tagged as "Rebel" with a Southern German accent.

In our barracks were two Jewish enlistees from Brooklyn, I don't remember their names; a Chicago guy, Donald Sonnenfeld, who became my best friend; Mel Stahler from Scranton, Pennsylvania; and Phillip Marino, a rather chubby guy from St. Paul, Minnesota who occupied the bunk next to mine.

On the first Friday we were there, training was cut short. We were told to be in our barracks for a big "party," and while we were sure it wasn't a real party, we knew to expect something unusual. To our surprise, our corporal explained what the party was all about.

We were ordered to clear out the entire barracks of footlockers, duffle bags and bedding—everything. Then, they handed us scrub brushes, buckets and G.I. soap, and we were ordered to scrub the whole barracks from bottom to top. After we finished, our company commander checked our work, including the shine of our boots. Miraculously, we must have passed muster because in a few minutes, much to our relief, the "party" was over.

But, when they had nothing else for us to do, this routine became *the* routine for the next five weeks until we completed basic. Daytimes were always busy but in the evening until bedtime, our time was our own and free. Free except that we were only allowed to go to the base theater and/or the bowling alley. I was bored. I could take only so much bowling, and the movie was always a rerun. I was anxious to get out of there for some real R&R.

This is when I tried my hand at boxing. I never wanted to be a prize fighter but they told us that anyone who volunteered to be on the base boxing team was excused from regular training. That sounded good to me so I reported to the gym to train with other volunteer boxers.

I weighed 150 pounds, which placed me in the middleweight class. After the third Friday of training, the coach pronounced me ready for the base boxing matches that were held every Friday night at the outdoor arena.

I wasn't scared and for my first fight, I was matched against a tall Texan who also weighed 150 pounds. But he had height to his advantage—he was at least 6-feet tall and I was 5 feet, 3 inches. (I grew another two-and-a-half inches within the next two years, but not soon enough to help me then when I needed the height the most.)

But there I was—all 5 feet 3 inches of me in the boxing ring. The bell rang for the two of us to meet in ring center, and after hearing the referee's instructions we came out swinging. I don't remember much after meeting my opponent in the center of the ring. All I know is I was knocked out in the first 15 seconds. Not only was I knocked out, my nose was broken. They had to carry me off amidst the roar of cheers, shouts and jeers. No more boxing for Private Henry Schuster.

While we were all anxious to fight the dirty Gerries, we found that anti-Semitism was alive and well in places outside Nazi Germany. Even in America, many Jews were afraid of letting anyone know they were Jewish. About two weeks after we got to basic, my bunk neighbor had a confession to make. He was in tears when he explained that the C on his dog tag was wrong. He told me he was really Jewish and had not wanted to admit it because he was afraid of discrimination. His father was Italian, probably Catholic, and his mother was Jewish, but the entire family lived a Jewish life. He was bar mitzvahed and attended Hebrew school. Mel, Donald and I urged him to see Chaplain Goldstein and ask for help. He did, and no big deal was made of it. His dog tags were changed within days.

I considered myself a good soldier. I even liked Army food. That was probably because of my background in the children's homes where the food was always cafeteria style and probably not the best. And Aunt Perle wasn't the best of cooks, either. So, Army cooking was fine by me.

I also excelled on the rifle range where I was given the highest rating and was awarded an "Expert" medal. I loved Army life and was happy to be on the go all the time. But something felt wrong. During this time, I was painfully aware that I was different from the other guys in that I was not a real American citizen, a fact that bothered me so much that after Friday night services, I spoke to the chaplain about it. As soon as he could, he made arrangements with the base adjutant to get the required papers. Soon, the paperwork came through and I filled them out. I was well on my way to becoming an American citizen.

KP duty is something every soldier has to endure during his army life. Shortly before leaving Shepherd Field, I was on dishwasher duty with several other guys. My job was to carry a tray full of cups across the kitchen over to the dishwasher. Instead of lugging the tray across the room, I thought it would be more fun to throw the cups one-by-one to the guy loading the machine. The mess sergeant took a dim view of shenanigans like that.

"Stop that, Schuster! Don't be such a lazy cuss. Do it right!" he yelled. I was having too much fun to stop, so I kept throwing cups. My buddy, the "catcher" at the dishwasher, was laughing so hard he dropped the next cup; it hit the cement floor and smashed into a thousand pieces. Now, the sergeant was really steamed.

"That will cost you, Schuster!" he screamed at me. I shrugged it off. What could he do? It was just a lousy cup. I forgot about it and wouldn't think about it again until my discharge when I was told to pay up for destroying government property or I wouldn't be released from military service. The army has a long memory. Much longer than mine.

I wasn't at Shepherd Field very long when I was transferred to Truax Field in Madison, Wisconsin. Luckily, or maybe it wasn't luck, my Jewish friends were included in the transport, which was the Air Corps. training center for radio repair school. A second group went to Scott Field in Illinois to be trained as radio operators, and a third group was transferred to gunnery school.

For the first week, the only daily duty we had was an hour's worth of physical training, or just PT as we called it. After PT, we were free to do whatever we wanted. The University of Wisconsin had a campus on base, and I enrolled in a couple of courses that took up another hour each afternoon. We were bored with so much free time on our hands so when a public bus route was established from the base into Madison, we boarded with the expectation of living it up in the big city. A roundtrip ticket only cost a nickel, so we were able to go often.

Our high expectations of Madison's delights were warranted. Madison was a great town for servicemen, and the Madison people were warm and friendly. All movies were free for servicemen, and complete strangers invited us to their homes for dinner. The war brought all Americans together, and servicemen were held in particularly high esteem.

For other entertainment, the USO sponsored several servicemen's clubs where guys could meet girls for dancing, and there was always one guy in the crowd who could play the piano. The hottest number then was "Boogie Woogie Bugle Boy of Company B."

Milwaukee is only 60 miles from Madison, and my buddies and I would catch the train at the base and take it to Milwaukee for the day. Milwaukee was the greatest servicemen's town in the USA. The Milwaukee citizens turned a blind eye to underage military personnel drinking beer. Everybody in the military, no matter what their age, was allowed to drink 3.2 beer and several breweries established clubs for military personnel only. The beer was free, too. I didn't drink, then, so I couldn't take advantage of the free booze. I came from a non-drinking family. Certain Orthodox Jews don't believe in drinking alcoholic beverages—my family being a part of that group. Nor did I like the taste. I would grow to like it later, however, at least enough to drink it. It's still something I can live without.

Once my buddy, Phillip Mathews, who had a beautiful singing voice and was a tenor in the famous San Francisco Opera company, and I went to a USO club in downtown Milwaukee where a national USO troupe, one of many that toured the military bases to entertain the troops, was entertaining with a live national radio broadcast. The star of the show was Joy Hamilton, a famous entertainer and singer in her day. Joy asked for volunteers to be a part of the show, and since Phil was a professional opera singer, he and a sailor teamed up and sang arias from "Carmen."

Then, Joy asked if there was anyone else who had talent, and Phil told her that while his buddy (me) was talent-free, I was a German refugee and had only been in this country for three years. Joy thought that would be of interest to the rest of the country, so she interviewed me on the radio. When I spoke, she remarked that I had a Southern accent and asked me how come. I told her I was from South Germany. It got a big laugh.

Back at Truax, our instructor, Mr. Bard, was an easygoing, middle-aged civilian electrical engineer who was 4-F, that is, not able to perform as a soldier because of a malformed arm. All the classes were held in the same classroom, a room with a wall of cabinets with sliding doors and a stone top. The room came equipped with hand tools that included a soldering iron, pliers and VTM meter (a volt ohm meter with capability to measure current) as well as an oscilloscope.

Classroom work came easily to me, and I'm proud to say I was always the best student in the class. It's a good thing I knew the material, because once I went to St. Paul to visit a buddy and partied hearty, as they say. When I got back to the base, I hadn't had any sleep for nearly 24 hours and in class could hardly keep my eyes open. Seeing my predicament, Bard took pity on me and told me to crawl into the cabinet with the sliding doors and go to sleep. I did, and was quickly snoring.

When they woke me for chow three hours later, I felt so much better, but I had been in such a crouched position for so long that, for the first few minutes, I couldn't stand. Finally, feeling returned to my arms and legs, and I hobbled off to the mess hall none the worse for wear.

At long last, my wish to become an American citizen was to come true. Sometime in September, I was told to bring two witnesses and see a federal judge to be sworn in. Because I was an American high school graduate, I didn't have to take the usual American history test. All I had to do was raise my right hand and repeat the judge's words. With two soldiers as witnesses, I was now a full-fledged American citizen. It was the proudest day of my life, and my joy must have shown on my face because the judge insisted on taking the three of us to lunch. I don't remember what I ate, but it was the best lunch I ever had.

It was autumn, and for the Jewish High Holidays, Jewish soldiers were allowed to attend services at the local synagogue where the rabbi welcomed us all. Families were encouraged to befriend military personnel over the holidays and girl of 16 or 17 attached herself to me immediately. I could tell she had a crush on me when she invited me to her home for dinner. While I was grateful that she and her family befriended me, I was not interested in being her boyfriend so I kept my distance during the evening. I think she got the message without being hurt. Even if I had been interested in a relationship, this was no time to get involved. Being a soldier in peacetime makes relationships difficult. During wartime, the circumstances make it nearly impossible.

Winter rolled over Wisconsin like a steamroller, and the first snowfall was so bad it made Wisconsin record books. Snow drifted so deeply at both ends of the barracks we couldn't open the doors. Somehow, we were able to push open a window and crawl out onto a snow bank. Finding shovels somewhere, it took us the better part of the morning to dig out the barracks doorways.

I was always cold—colder than I had ever been in a German winter, and the two heating stoves in the barracks did little more than keep us from freezing. We tried to keep the fire from dying down by taking turns tending it and stoking wood into it to keep it going throughout the night.

Because Truax Field was established strictly for World War II, the barracks were put up cheaply and fast and lacked even the most basic amenities. Each barrack had two wood-fire stoves for heat, but insulation was thin if there was insulation at all. I remember being happy my bunk was on top because heat rises, and I figured it would be warmer there. Every bunk was occupied except the bunk under mine. Having so many people in the barracks meant that the soldiers' body also added to the warmth. Body heat was also sometimes generated in that one vacant bunk, a bunk that was reserved for the occasional hooker who could be sneaked on base for a few hours—and a few bucks.

I can still feel that Wisconsin cold. It was so cold that one Saturday, a group of us attended a Wisconsin University football game. The temperature must have been zero that day, even in the sun, and not a single guy stayed around for the second half. Back at the barracks, we returned to frozen latrine pipes. Just to go to the john we had to walk a block in the freezing cold.

That year, there were snowdrifts everywhere that hid ditches and gullies. From the bus stop to our barracks, there was a little bridge over a deep ditch. Returning to the barracks one night, one soldier had a few too many and he missed the bridge completely. He tried to cross over through the snowdrift that covered the ditch and went waist-deep in snow. He was so drunk he just collapsed into the softness and lay there singing. His singing was how we found him since we couldn't see him. If he hadn't been singing, he would have frozen to death.

The worst thing about the Wisconsin winter was that we had to wear our olive-drab uniforms—made from wool. I still couldn't wear wool next to my body and not only were the uniforms made of wool, but so was the Army-issue long underwear. Remembering how I handled the wool problem when I was younger, I went to Madison and bought a pair of pajamas. Instead of underwear, I wore the soft cotton pajamas. But I wasn't the only one. Another fellow in our barracks wore pajamas—not under his wool uniform, but at night. In a world where everyone slept in his underwear, this guy's pink pajamas were the outfit's laughing stock. It didn't seem to bother him though as he always wore his "jimmies" proudly.

The war in Europe was not going well, and our troops found stiff German resistance in Belgium. New troops were needed and half the soldiers in our barracks were yanked out of school and transferred to the Army infantry. I was disappointed when I wasn't chosen and had to continue radio school. I was itching to go to Germany and fight the Nazis.

But with those men gone, another company's men were transferred into our barracks. Two bunks down from me was a fellow by the name of Zimmermann, an ardent anti-Semite who always tried to engage Jewish soldiers in what he called "dialogues." Among the lies he told was his favorite: the one where Jews used a portion of the circumcised foreskin to make soup that the family had to drink. He said he was very sure of this since he had once attended a circumcision.

Another tale he told was that matzo was made with Christian blood. Eventually, all the guys in the barracks figured he was a loud-mouthed jerk and ostracized him for his wild stories. In fact, one of our non-Jewish friends challenged him to a fight with most of us lining up behind just itching to get a piece of him.

At Christmas in most American venues, Jews often volunteer to work in the place of Christians so they can celebrate their special holiday with friends and family. The military is no different, and we Jewish boys volunteered for KP so that our non-Jewish soldiers could celebrate their holiday. It was the least we could do to pay them back for their support against the anti-Semites in Europe—as well as in our own barracks.

The war raged on in Europe but in Wisconsin we had time on our hands. I was itching to fight the Germans, but no dice. So, I kept busy as best I could and did part-time work when it was available.

The Oscar Meyer Company had a meat packing plant in Madison that employed me and several other soldiers with Sunday jobs. I worked the hot dog machine, and after the first week of watching how hot dogs were made, I no longer wanted to look at hot dogs, let alone eat one. Another Sunday, I worked as a pin boy at the base bowling alley. After the umpteenth pin flew up and hit me, I decided that was the end of my pin boy career. I would have been safer in the frontlines at Normandy.

All this while, I had not been in touch with any of the kids from the German or French orphanages or the ship to America, but I knew that Elfriede Meyer, the girl I had loved so deeply as a child in Europe and who sailed with me from France to New York, had been sent to Chicago. I contacted the Chicago HIAS office to ask if they knew who Elfriede Meyer was or where she might be. After several phone calls, I was finally connected to someone who found her records and gave me her address.

I contacted Elfriede after a few quick phone calls. I think she was so shocked that it was really me on the other end of the line that she had little to say. But I managed to make a date with her. As a child, I had been hopelessly in love with the beautiful Elfriede, and I know Elfriede felt the same way about me. Shy children that we were, we never told each other.

I couldn't wait to see her, and the next weekend standing at the station in the deep Wisconsin winter, I anxiously awaited the train that would take me from Madison to Chicago, and to Elfriede. It was only 90 miles, so it wouldn't be long before I was with her. Thoughts raced through my head with overlapping images of Elfriede laughing, Elfriede looking down at me as I rested my head in her lap; Elfriede running through the fields near the school. Would I know her? How would she look? Would she still be as pretty as she had been years before? Would she be disappointed when she saw me? Had I changed? Would she like me still?

I saw her before she saw me. She was standing on the platform looking at each person as they descended from the train. Slender and pretty, she had developed from a beautiful child to a beautiful woman. She had been a kid when I last saw her; now, she was a woman. I was enthralled.

At last, I was able to work my way through the passengers and off the train. Our eyes met, and we fell into each other's arms. Her perfume filled my senses. It was so good to see her again. We hugged for a long, long time, all the while babbling to each other in English, German and French. My heart was bursting I was so happy.

After checking into the Stevens Hotel, an establishment taken over by the military for soldier R&R stays, we spent the whole next day together, and that evening we went to Chicago's famous Trianon Ballroom where Dinah Shore was singing with a big band. The Trianon Ballroom opened in 1922, was billed as one of Chicago's most opulent

ballrooms and had a Louis XVI-style décor. Its dance floor was immense and could accommodate roughly 3,000 dancers. I had never seen anything like it—it was magical. We danced and talked all night, and the next night I took her to her high school prom.

When I picked her up, she looked like she just stepped out of my dreams. We talked the whole night through, catching up on our own lives and the lives of some of the kids we knew in Germany and France and with whom she was in contact.

I told her about the rough time I had had with Aunt Perle, and she told me that she, too, had had a rough time of it emotionally. With no family in America to go to, the Joint Distribution Committee placed her in a foster home with people who wanted her only for the money they were given for her care. With no love or concern for her, they had treated her badly. I found out that during the war, many American families volunteered to become foster parents for the money they were given, and many of the children they fostered were abused both mentally and physically. Elfriede was one of those children.

I told Elrfriede about two boys we knew, also our siblings as we called all the kids from the orphanage, who were sent to a foster home in St. Louis where, luckily, they were welcomed warmly and were treated with love and kindness. It wasn't until after the war, however, when their trouble began. The boys' German parents had both survived the camps and were able to get to St. Louis to claim their children. By this time, the boys were in their teens and could hardly remember a life before they came to the foster home let alone their biological parents. Once again, the boys were uprooted, an event so stressful that one of the boys couldn't handle the separation from the only parents he had ever known and had to be placed in a mental institution. One of the things he said to some friends was that he just couldn't cope with calling these strangers father and mother.

Relating the story about the boys put a gloom on my time with Elfriede, but not for long. I loved being with Elfriede who was always so sweet and cheerful, and I wanted to stay with her. But duty called, and the next day I returned to the base. My leave was over.

On January 6, 1945, the Russians liberated 80,000 Jews in Budapest. On January 14, 1945, Russian troops invaded eastern Germany, and on January 18, 1945 the Nazis opened the Auschwitz gates and freed 66,000

Jews just before the arrival of the Russian troops. It has been estimated that two million people, a million and a half of that number being Jews, were put to death there.

Sometime toward the end of January 1945, those of us who had graduated radio school were transferred to Chanute Field at Rantoul/Champaign in Illinois. I was one of the graduates, and at Chanute Field we were instructed in physics, leaning towards radio and radar theory.

It was almost as cold in Illinois as it had been in Wisconsin, and the cold kept me indoors most of the time. But winter was easier in Illinois because the buildings were permanent, including the barracks, and were made of brick. It might have been as cold as in Wisconsin, but the brick buildings kept in the heat and we were warm, at least when we were indoors.

In 1945, Chanute was a rehabilitation center for returning air personnel, many of whom had chalked up a lot of missions over Germany. With combat duty so fresh in their minds, many took what they called army "chicken shit" rules less than seriously, and clashes were bound to happen.

Our PT instructor, a by-the-book sergeant with no combat experience, took us out on a physical exercise run one morning that led to a grassy area with "Keep off the grass" signs everywhere. Even though it was winter and the grass was brown, we were still expected to obey the signs. When two fellows dressed in fatigues with no insignias walked across the lawn, Sergeant By-the-Book came unglued and halted the run.

"What the hell do you think you're doing," he yelled at the perpetrators. "Can't you read? Just who do you think you are?"

"A piano player in a whorehouse," cracked one of the perps.

"What's your name?" responded red-faced Sarge with a surliness reserved for only the lowest-of-the-low rule breakers.

As it turned out, one was a lieutenant colonel, the other a major. Both had flown more than 100 missions over Germany as a B-17 bombardier, pilot and navigator. Meekly, in very low tones, Sarge apologized. Returning to us, we continued the rest of run in silence.

By 1945, I was able to find out that many of my relatives had escaped Germany by whatever means possible and by whatever route. I was in Champaign, Illinois when I found out my cousin Kathryn and her husband Leo had escaped and had made their way to Peoria where they now owned and operated a liquor store.

As luck would have it, Peoria was only 50 or 60 miles away. The first chance I got, I hitchhiked to Peoria for a weekend with Leo and Kathryn, a time we spent catching up, Kathryn filling me in on all she knew about others in the family. She knew about many relatives, but there still was no word about my mother and sisters.

When we ran out of things to talk about, Kathryn thought I might be up for some fun so she said she wanted to take me out for a night on the town. She and her husband took me to a nightclub called the Talk of the Town. Neither Kathryn nor Leo went out much, and neither knew the Talk of the Town was a strip joint. I don't think they wanted to admit their blunder, and both acted like they knew it all the time. I thought it was a great show and couldn't have been more pleased with their selection.

The highlight of the evening was when the hatcheck girl gave me a note from a young woman at the bar. The note said she wanted to meet me, and Kathryn, naïve as she was, assumed the girl was a USO girl. So did I, and I couldn't wait to meet her. She was a pretty, highly made-up young woman, and much as I would have liked to spend time with her, I explained I was with my cousins that evening. Not wanting to miss out on a good thing, I told her my buddy and I could come back the following weekend if she could get a friend. I must have been as naïve as my cousin because, flattered by her attention, I didn't realize the woman was a call girl. She must have been laughing up her sleeve when she made a date to meet at the club because the following Saturday, my buddy, Monahan, and I hitched to Peoria. Once in the club, we found a table and waited for our dates. After waiting several hours, even we realized we had been had. Peoria had a wild reputation; we should have known.

After our six-week stay at Chanute, we were on our way to Florida with a layover in St. Louis and Mobile, Alabama. During the Mobile layover, one of my buddies called his sister who lived in Mobile who came to the train station to see him. It was rumored she was married to Mickey Rooney, but I never heard her name, and I have no idea which number wife she was.

Chapter
FIFTEEN

"It was…America's third year in World War II. While I was in high school, the army was ensconced in virtually every hotel in Miami Beach. They had commandeered almost four hundred of them to house the thousands of servicemen being trained under the palm trees and along the pristine beaches to go to war. The U.S. military had taken over paradise, and there was no room for tourists."—Barbara Walters "Audition, A Memoir"

We arrived in Miami in great shape due to the fact that on the way we had semi-luxurious accommodations that included Pullman berths. From Miami, we were to go to a base in Boca Raton, but when we got there they wouldn't let us in because one of our guys had the mumps. He looked like he was doing a chipmunk imitation.

But what a break that was! Because of the mumps we were placed in the requisitioned Boca Club, a private country club that was the most luxurious in that part of Florida. It was a club so snobby it was restricted, meaning no Jews, Blacks or Asians. It made us, the Jewish soldiers, elated because we were there, and they could do nothing about it. Hooray for the good old US Army!

This was like a vacation. The food was scrumptious; the beds had crisp, clean white sheets that they changed daily. We felt wonderful with all that high living. Right on the beach, we had no duty and spent most of our time sunbathing. Unfortunately, it only lasted two weeks, and the lucky bastards who had the mumps were able to remain another two weeks.

Radar, the secret weapon of that time, was developed by the Bendix Corp. and initially the U.S. War Department had no interest in it. The big brains in the Pentagon thought it would never work. Consequently, Bendix sold it to Britain, an easier sale because the Brits could see its potential during the German Blitz. After the Brits made it work, the U.S. wanted it for the Air Force, but because the Brits now owned it, the US had to pay a heavy royalty to get it.

Once in our hands, our assignment was to learn how to install, tune, maintain and operate radar for our bombers. It was used for defensive as well as offensive purposes in all our B-25s, B-26s, B-17s, B-24s and later in the B-29s. Now, the Air Corps. no longer depended on the Norton Bomb Site for all our bombers.

Work was work, but play was play, and every weekend possible the Boca soldiers hitchhiked on U.S. 1 to Miami. With so many USOs in Miami Beach, it was a soldier's mecca. For Jewish soldiers, the YMHA was always a good place for dancing, fraternizing and eating. The Y was open to all denominations.

For Passover Seder in 1945, my good friend, Melvin Stahler, and I were invited to the home of an elderly couple by the name of Rose. Mrs. Rose told us that Mr. Rose's son was the famous Billy Rose. I had no idea who Billy Rose was, but Mel was impressed so I acted impressed too so as not to offend anyone. The Passover seder was great, and the house was exquisite. Who knew from Billy Rose?

It was about this time that I learned that my mother's sister, Matilde, had gotten out of Germany and was living in Jacksonville.

I didn't have her address, so I sent a telegram to my Uncle Solli in New York. He wired back with her address, and I decided that the next weekend I would hitchhike to Jacksonville.

I had no idea that Jacksonville was 400 miles from Miami, but I was lucky. While standing at a bus stop, a semitrailer truck stopped and the driver asked, "Anyone going to Jacksonville?" I yelled back that was where I wanted to go. He told me it would take at least eight hours and in case I wanted to sleep, I should crawl into the sleeping part of the rig, which I did. It was so comfortable, I fell asleep immediately, and the next thing I knew he was shaking me and inviting me for breakfast at a truck stop on U.S. 1 on the outskirts of Daytona Beach.

He dropped me off at the USO center in Jacksonville Beach where I asked a stranger how to get to Gilmore Street. The man said it would be easy to find because he would drive me there. And he did.

Today, it's hard to remember how kind people were in those days. Unlike the Vietnam era, then people were especially kind to servicemen and women. I am pleased and proud that the U.S. servicemen and servicewomen who have served and are serving in the Middle East today are treated with the same respect as the World War II servicemen. They deserve it.

Once at my Aunt Matilde's house, I rang the doorbell, and shortly a nice-looking young woman answered the door. By the way she was dressed, I took her for the maid doing her house cleaning chores.

"Excuse me, does the Hirsch family live here?" I asked, to which she promptly responded that her parents lived next door in the other half of the duplex. When I told her who I was, she hugged me and kissed me, explaining that she was my first cousin Martha, and that I also had a cousin Ilse, her sister. Excited and overwhelmed, Martha, her 2-year-old daughter, Edna, and I hurried next door to see Aunt Matilde.

I would have known her anywhere even after all these years. Tante Matilde was two years older then my mother, but she looked and sounded so much like my mother they could have been twins. The emotion was so intense, she started to cry. She dearly loved my mother and wanted to know what I knew about her in Germany.

I still didn't know the full extent of the Holocaust nor what had happened to my mother and sisters. I was still under the impression my mother and sisters were working at the old age home and were fine. I told her as much as I knew, which regrettably wasn't current information. I still carry the guilt of not having written more so I could keep up with what was happening. I keep thinking that, maybe, if I had known what kind of trouble they were in I could have done something. Somehow, it might have been different.

Once we had settled in on her comfortable couch and had ice tea to drink and fresh-baked cookies to munch on, I heard their story. Tante Matilde's husband, Sigmund, had been a very successful businessman in Germany. But in 1939, Nazi laws took away his ability to make a living, so they reluctantly made plans to leave the country in which they had been born and raised. They were some of few in our family who were able to get out and immigrate to the U.S. But once here, with a limited command of the English language, Sigmund was unable to work in his profession. The 62-year-old man had to take a job as a fishmonger in a supermarket, a job he hated with a passion. But he could not afford to be choosey, and he was grateful that his son-in-law, Saul, who was the store's meat department manager, was able to get the job for him.

Another relative, Simon Landes, who was a very learned Jewish scholar, managed a liquor store. Many well-educated and successful European Jews had to take menial jobs after they fled Europe. That may be the reason why Jewish parents of that era stressed education for their children. A good education meant a good job—something the parents didn't have.

To get myself back to Boca, I planned to buy a bus ticket, and Saul volunteered to drive me to the station. A big mistake. Saul's downfall in life was that he was an incorrigible gambler, and on the way to the bus he told me to come with him so he could introduce me to a friend of his.

We stopped in a sleazy part of town at a building that was equally sleazy and walked up the stairs to a loft. When my eyes adjusted to the dim light, I saw that it was an illegal gambling hall. I got fidgety, worried I'd miss my bus, but Saul told me to relax, and that he'd make sure I got back to the base on time.

He played game after game of poker while I anxiously watched the game as well as my watch. It was getting later and later, and there was no time now to get to the bus before it left. Finally, seeing my panic he quit playing, and we piled into his car. Instead of the bus station, he took me to the airport. There, he bought me a plane ticket to Fort Lauderdale (Saul had had a good day at the poker table), and I arrived at the base just in the nick of time.

On April 15, 1945, British troops liberated Bergen-Belsen. British military reports stated that "…both inside and outside the huts was a carpet of dead bodies, human excreta, rags and filth."

With my newly refound family, instead of going to Miami on the weekends, I now went to Jacksonville, and as often as I could. It was April of 1945. Before the war ended, we knew very little about the German death camps. I always hoped and wished for the very best for my mother and sisters' lives, but I had not gotten any letters or heard anything about them since 1942. I knew about the concentration camps, but we still thought they were only for the men. My father died before the war began, so I had no worry there, and I was under the impression that Mother, Bertel and Margot were safe and still living in Frankfurt.

The tide had turned, and the war in Europe was now going well for the Allies. American troops were fighting on German soil, and the British had already reached the town of Bergen-Belsen in northern Germany. To their horror, they discovered one of many concentration camps, and what they found was just as inconceivable as the horrors the Russians found at Auschwitz-Birkenau. Bergen-Belsen was a carbon copy of Auschwitz with thousands of bodies piled high ready for disposal. It was inconceivable that any of the prisoners would be found alive, but they were. Many were close to death and would not live to see freedom. Others lived and wished they had not. The horror of it was in their eyes.

I didn't know it at the time, but my sister, Bertel, was one of the Bergen-Belsen survivors, and the only one of my immediate family to live—if you could call it that. She was among the living dead, technically alive but almost a skeleton from being starved and slowly dying from malnutrition and typhus. Her recovery would take months.

But during her recovery, somehow she learned that an American newspaperman was traveling with the British troops, and from her bed she struggled to find someone who would bring him to her. When he arrived, she told him that she had a brother living in the United States. She remembered my address, and desperate that she find me before she died, asked for his help in getting word to her baby brother Heinz Schuster.

The Associated Press reporter contacted his newspaper, and the paper, in turn, contacted radio station KWKH in Shreveport. The station manager immediately contacted Sam Schuster, asking him if he had any knowledge of a young man by the name of Heinz Schuster.

Sam immediately contacted the Boca Raton Air Base, and the information about my sister worked its way to my company's orderly room. I wasn't there; I was in Miami and didn't return until the middle of the night. Arriving back at Boca, I found a note pinned to my bunk ordering me to report to the officer of the day. I assumed that I had done something wrong. Maybe they thought I was AWOL. Who knew? So, it wasn't until 2 a.m. Monday that I reported to the office as ordered.

Saluting, I asked what it was all about and was handed a note telling me to call Shreveport, no matter what time it was. My first thought was that something happened to someone at Sam's house. Using the official phone, I made the call.

Hearing Sam's voice put me at ease. At least *he* was okay. He quickly told me about the message he had gotten from the people at the radio station. I couldn't believe my ears. My mother or one of my sisters was alive! But, which one? What could I do to get to her? What could I do to help her?

I was overwhelmed not only with joy but with fear. I knew my surviving relative, whoever she was, was in bad shape—possibly dying—and I was afraid I wouldn't get to her in time. I couldn't sleep, and the night seemed eons long. But, I had to wait until daylight to do anything at all.

Should I call one of my cousins or go to Shreveport myself? I decided it would be better if I went to Washington D.C. to try to find out more. Who had been liberated? Bertel? Margot or Mother? I asked for and was granted a 10-day emergency leave.

In Washington, I first went to the State Department for information only to find that none was available. However, a young Jewish-German immigrant who was working at the State Department as a military attaché was sympathetic and told me to arrange to have an affidavit of support ready just in case she lived and could be transported out of Germany, which I did.

Next, I went to the American Red Cross for help—a huge mistake. No help was offered, and in addition to offering no help they offered no sympathy. The attitude was, "So what's the big deal that someone survived?" I felt angry as well as totally alone and helpless.

Then, I remembered that Colonel Robert Lyons was now living in the Washington D.C. area. After having served in Europe, he and his family moved to a house in Newport News, Virginia. When I called, Betty answered, and I explained the situation to her. She instructed me to come to their house, and from there I was able to contact other family members nearby. My next stop was New York get whatever help I could from my other cousins. Everyone volunteered to have whoever had been liberated come live with them. If we could ever get her to America, she had a place to live, and a family to love and take care of her.

From Baltimore, I took a train to New York to see cousins Milan and Mina, and Milan's mother, Aunt Rosa. We were incredibly aware of how lucky we were that even one person in my family had survived. The ordeal, though painful, pulled the family together. Wishing to give me something else to think about on my trip back, Mina's daughter, Ina, gave me the book, "Forever Amber" as a going-away present. With no time or inclination to read it then, I stuffed it into my duffle bag and boarded the train back to Boca. The book was a racy book for the time, and one she thought, as a young serviceman, I might find intriguing. If nothing more, she thought it might take my mind off my problems.

CHAPTER
SIXTEEN

My hope was that I would somehow get news directly from my family in Germany, but time passed with no new information. It was now August, and back at the base we were preparing for graduation. It was then that I got a letter that had been forwarded to me from Shreveport. It had a London postmark and had been in the mail for more than four weeks. It had come to me in a round about way—via a British soldier who had been given the letter by my sister who then forwarded it to his mother in England. She, in turn, mailed it to me in Shreveport. Now, I knew who had survived. Bertel was alive and on her way to recovery.

Happy as I was to know Bertel had lived, I was devastated to learn that my mother and Margot had not. Knowing that I would never see Margot or Mother again—ever—was almost more pain than I could bear. I think I was able to survive it only because Bertel was still alive. I have never known such pain and joy at the same time.

When I finally got to see Bertel, she told me some of what had happened, but only as much as she could bear to talk about. It would be another 50 years before she could open up, 50 years before she could come to grips with the horror she had witnessed.

What she could tell me then was that when she, Margot and Mother were at the old age home, they were safe; they stayed there until 1942 and then everything changed. They were deported. First, they were put on a train to Berlin and then herded into cattle cars to be taken to Estonia. The cattle cars were so crowded no one could sit or even turn around. The sheer pressure of bodies kept everyone upright. There were no bathroom facilities, so excrement fouled the car floors as well as shoes, legs and clothing. Once at their destination, SS men, holding riding crops, evaluated each woman. With the crop, one of the SS men pointed to the left or right as each woman emerged from the cattle car. They didn't know it at the time, but those sent to the right would live. Those sent to the left would not.

Bertel, a young healthy woman, was deemed strong enough for continued labor and was sent to the right. Mother, a heavyset woman in her late 40s, was deemed not strong enough for hard labor, so not useful and sent to the left. Margot, who had a limp from a badly set broken leg as a teenager, was deemed not useful as well, and she also was directed to go to the left. Later, those on the left were herded onto a bus, a bus that strangely, had no windows. It wasn't a bus at all, but a mobile gas chamber. The bus motor was started, but the wheels didn't move. The buses' exhaust fumes were being piped into the passenger compartment. It wasn't long before all the passengers were dead. My mother and sister were dead.

For the next several weeks I corresponded with Bertel in the same manner as her first letter to me, only in reverse. My letters first went to a woman I didn't know in London who then forwarded them to my sister in Germany.

There was nothing I could do for my sister, and I still had a job to do as a soldier. It would be months before I could get Bertel out of Germany and into the United States, so in the interim, as hard as it was, I made myself put the Bertel situation on a back burner, and

I concentrated on my own life until such time as I was able to get to her.

I remember it was hurricane season in Boca, and a huge storm was predicted for the region. Our barracks were flimsy wooden structures, so we were moved to the more substantial officers' quarters. During the three-day stay in the O Q, I finally got around to reading "Forever Amber." Ina was right. It was the diversion I needed.

After the hurricane, we graduated and were all promoted to the rank of corporal, and the entire class of 30 men got orders to report to Williams Field in Chandler, Ariz. But first, we were allowed a 10-day leave of absence before we were required to report for duty. Because I knew that Bertel would go to New York to stay with relatives once she was able to travel and once she had permission to enter the United States, I decided to go to New York. There, I made plans for her arrival and helped in the preparations for her immigration.

My 10-day leave of absence over, I returned to Williams Field, a permanent air base that was much more convenient than Boca Raton or Texas. It was August and extremely hot, and I was used to hot weather having lived in Louisiana and Florida. But the 120-degree Arizona heat was different than anything I had ever experienced. Happily, we had no duty and were able to loaf, doing whatever we wanted. With nothing better to do, two of my buddies and I went to the flight line to ask if we could hitch a flight to somewhere—anywhere. We didn't care. Anywhere out of Chandler. A friendly sergeant, a flight engineer, invited us to join his flight to Lowery Field just east of Denver. He instructed us to pack dress clothes, khakis and dress shoes since the plane would be in Colorado for two days. After clearing it with our officer in charge, we hopped aboard.

Coming in for a landing at Lowery, another plane approached the runway at the same time as ours, and an argument ensued between our pilot and the pilot of the other plane as to who had the right to land first. Interestingly, I again rubbed elbows, or in this case wings, with another famous personality. We found out later that the C-47 that wanted our landing space was piloted by none other than Flying Sergeant Gene Autry.

Once we landed, a bus carried us to the control tower, and a flight controller and staff sergeant mentioned that he was going to Denver for the day with an overnight stay. Inviting us to join him, my buddy and I jumped into the rumble seat of his 1932 Model A Ford. During the ride, we were having a great time laughing and singing when all at once a wheel whizzed past us on the road.

"That poor sucker lost a wheel," we yelled, laughing 'till our sides hurt. But, within seconds, we stopped laughing. Our Model A went down hard, with a thump. Climbing out, we were found the wheel in a ditch, but there was no jack anywhere in the car. In desperation, the four of us manually lifted the left side of the car off the ground and reattached the wheel by using one nut from each of the three other wheels. Though crippled, the car made it into Denver.

Once there, we found a Christian-operated service club where we were treated royally. Serving us coffee and donuts, a young lady asked if we were saved. I had no idea what she was talking about, but she was pretty and I didn't want to disappoint her so I agreed to be saved. It didn't take long until I found out what it meant to be "saved," and when I did I told her I was Jewish. She replied, "That doesn't matter." I was Jewish in my heart and soul and strongly believed intellectually in my religion, but I figured what the hell? If it paid for my donut and coffee, I would agree to be saved. It meant absolutely nothing to me, but it sure made her happy.

On the flight back to Williams, the pilot mentioned that later in the afternoon our plane would make a detour to March Field in

Southern California for a short stay. I was under the impression we were going to Los Angeles, so I stayed with the plane for the trip. March Field was nothing like I thought Los Angeles would be like. It was just as hot as it was in Arizona with just as much barren desert, so I decided I wouldn't like living in Los Angeles. Years later, I found out that we were in Riverside, well inland of Los Angeles and a lot hotter than the famed Los Angeles and Hollywood.

Within a few days or so we were told that our entire group would be shipped to Fort Lewis, Washington, then shipped from Seattle to the Philippines, news I didn't take well. I desperately wanted to get to Europe to be with Bertel, so I asked the base chaplain for his help to have my orders changed. I even asked to see the base commander to get his help. Neither could do anything for me.

Going to the Philippines was so upsetting I told my story to anyone who would listen on the off-chance someone would hear it who could help. Nothing. Friday, the ship-out day, was fast approaching. Desperate to try anything, on Tuesday evening I called Sam Schuster in Shreveport to see if with his political connections, he could help change my orders. That worked. It turned out that Sam was a personal friend of both Senator Ellender and Congressman Overton Brooks of Louisiana, whom I subsequently learned were persuaded by Sam to help change my orders. Both, I'm told, intervened directly with the Secretary of War. So on Friday morning, when our entire group was packed and ready to leave for the Philippines, one of my buddies ran up to me yelling that my name had been called over base public address system. I was to report to the officer in charge.

I was given a train ticket and all my records with orders to report to Selma Field in Monroe, Louisiana. That Friday afternoon I was on my way to Europe. I knew Sam's connection did the trick, and I was grateful.

After three weeks at Selma, I was assigned to an Army transport at Newport News, Virginia that headed for Le Havre, France. In Bertel's last letter, she wrote that she was trying to leave Germany for France. While still in Louisiana, I called my cousin, Leo Schwabacher, because I knew that his good friends, the Franks, lived in Paris. I asked Leo to write to the Franks to see if they could find my sister.

After a long search, they found her at a camp set up for liberated survivors. More than just locate her, they invited her and her friend, Ilse Wetterhahn, who had been at Bergen-Belsen concentration camp with her, to stay with them. Leo gave me the Franks' address.

Arriving at Le Havre, our transport ended up at a collecting base at Chateau Thierry. This was only temporary, and after a week I asked the officer in charge if he could give me a pass so I could get to Paris.

"No way," he replied. "Can't give you an official pass. But I could 'forget' to conduct roll call for the next three days if that would help. If you're gone, who'd be the wiser?"

With my barracks bag full of cigarettes, candy and all sorts of goodies I was able to buy at the PX, I left for Paris, 60 miles from our camp. The first 40 miles, I was able to hitchhike on an army 6x6 truck. The next two miles, I rode in the back of an oxcart. Then, I was able to flag down a freight train and ride in the steam engine with the engineer and the fireman to within three miles of Paris. I still spoke French pretty well, so once I arrived in Paris, I was able to ask directions. It only took three Metro trains to get me to the Franks' house.

I was beside myself, and I hoped it wasn't all a mistake. I hoped that the person staying with the Franks really was my sister.

I found the apartment house and scanned the directory on the ground floor. The Franks' apartment was on the third floor, it said. So, walking up the stairs, I stopped on what I thought was at the third floor, but name on the door was not Franks. I had forgotten that in Europe the first floor is called *parterre*. What in the United States would be considered the first floor was actually the second floor in Paris.

As I started toward the stairs, I heard voices coming from the stairwell, so I stayed on the landing of the "second" floor waiting for the people coming down to pass. I couldn't believe my eyes. There she was! My sister! It really was Bertel!

We fell into each other's arms, hugging and crying for what seemed like hours. I couldn't get close enough to her. I couldn't stop touching her for fear I'd lose her. I vowed I would never let her out of my sight again and tears streamed down our faces. We found each other at last. We found each other at last.

Bertel was thin and pale. She had been through so much and was still recovering from the after affects of typhus, a debilitating disease that is carried from one person to another by fleas or lice, both of which were rampant in the concentration camps. Fever, headache, weakness and muscle aches are common typhus symptoms, along with a rash and worse complications that include swelling of the heart as well as brain swelling—all fatal if not treated.

What she would, or could, tell me was that everyone in the camps had been cold and sick. Thin garments were not enough to keep already-emaciated bodies warm. Food was putrid, when there was food at all, and water was dredged from a pond in which dead Jewish bodies floated. Fifty years later, Bertel was finally able to talk about the horror. When she was able to open up, she spoke at colleges, high schools and in front of private groups, her agony somewhat relieved by the mere telling of the atrocities she had seen.

My heart ached for her and the millions of other Jews who had gone through her ordeal and worse. No one could have pried me away from her now, and I stayed with Bertel and Ilse for as long as I could before I had to return back to Chateau Theirry. We had so much to talk about. So much to catch up on. So many years lost we could never recover.

I had to tear myself away from Bertel and go back to Paris. I got back somehow; I really don't remember how I got back. I was so full of emotion it was all a blur. But I remember it was late in the evening. I was hungry, but the mess hall was closed, so I went back to my tent—now just wanting a good night's rest.

But, in the dim light, I saw someone lying in my bed. It was a French prostitute, whom I was told later, had done a brisk business earlier in the evening. She had crashed in my bunk when the guys were through with her. She wanted to stay and promised me a free trick if I would let her. I was exhausted and in no mood for her kind. After being with my sweet sister, this woman disgusted me, and I threw her out.

A week later, we were put into a 40 and 8 box car for Germany. Several of the officers were in a passenger car, but none of us knew where we were going. Some distance from Chateau Thierry, the train stopped and I heard my name called. Someone was looking for me to be a translator for one of the soldiers who had an appendicitis attack. I was to accompany him to a French hospital in Strasbourg to act as his interpreter. They gave me an official pouch with the service records for both him and for me, and I was told that in a few days another troop transport would pick us up.

The soldier had the emergency appendectomy performed and made it through the operation with flying colors. My services as an interpreter for the appendicitis case no longer required, I joined a British encampment that was stationed in Strasbourg. I would be able to stay with the Brits until the next troop of Americans picked me up.

The train for Germany was made up of mostly boxcars, and for comfort we were issued sleeping bags. The car's floor was covered with straw, and at one end was a so-called potty latrine. Not the Ritz, but good enough. As soon as we arrived steamed into Germany, the French train engines were exchanged for a German locomotive. It was bitterly cold and even though we had sleeping bags, we were shivered all night. I must have reverted to my native tongue to say a few choice swear words, and soon after crossing the border everyone knew I spoke German.

Nightfall came, and the train stopped at a German railway station for the track to be cleared for our train. While we waited, someone had the bright idea of getting a stove, which would keep us warm at night. The only stove we knew of was the one in the station master's office, and we figured since the station master probably wouldn't sell it to us, we'd have to steal it. Because I spoke German, I was requisitioned to go. The office was empty when we got there but the fire was till burning. We had to douse the fire in the stove to cool it and once it was cool enough to carry, we hauled it back to the train complete with a large supply of firewood and stovepipe.

I don't remember how we installed the stovepipe out of the car. I don't remember if it went through the roof or through the door. In any event, we did it, and we were much warmer and much happier that night. Unfortunately, the jostling of the train caused embers to fall out of the stove onto the straw and it ignited. I woke up to the sound of someone yelling, "Fire!" Sliding the door open, we kicked the stove, stove pipe and wood out the car. We were passing through a town at the time, and I can only hope the stove didn't set anything else on fire.

Later in the day, we arrived at the German town of Füerstenfeldbruck, which was our final destination. At Füerstenfeldbruck, we were billeted at a former Wehrmacht base. The American Red Cross installed a recreational center there that was manned by American women, but German girls were employed to serve coffee, donuts and ice cream. By that time, fraternization with the Germans was allowed.

At the recreation center, a cartoonist sat on a stool over in a corner and drew pencil sketches in exchange for cigarettes. I liked watching him work, so I sat beside him and we started to talk. He told me that his wife was Jewish and also was a Nazi victim, but whether he was telling me the truth or not I don't know. Most all Germans denied any involvement or sympathy with the Nazi regime once the war was over. People I *knew* were involved later swore innocence.

One of the young German girls who served coffee and donuts was surprised that I spoke German and asked me how come. I told her that I was born in Germany, and that I was Jewish. She touched my forehead and said that it could not be since I had no horns. They were taught that all Jews had horns. I gave her a short, but graphic, history lesson about what had been done to European Jews, especially German Jews. How could she not have known? How could she believe Jews had horns? Incredible.

Boys will be boys and while I was at the Red Cross, someone mentioned that in a neighboring town there were a lot of easy girls—something that almost always catches the attention of young, single enlisted men. So a group of us decided we should check it out. What did we have to lose?

We were told the village was within walking distance of Füerstenfeldbruck, but no one told us in what direction. Who cared? We decided there was no time like the present, so we started off in the direction we thought was the way. An hour went by and we still had not come to the town, By then, we figured we were lost. Then we noticed some lights about a half a mile in the distance, so we decided to follow the lights, see if there were people there and get directions on how to find our way back to our base. By now, no one had any interest in easy women even if they jumped out at us from the bushes.

As we approached the buildings that we thought were part of an American Army base, we found it was a former German army camp, and the troops occupying it now were not American. When they spoke to us, we quickly found out they couldn't speak English, and that they were Polish. My buddies suggested I speak German to them, thinking the languages might be close enough that they would understand. No sooner were the German words out of my mouth, when with motions, they ordered me to put my hands above my head and go with them. I found myself under arrest and placed in a tent occupied by what looked like an officer. I couldn't believe what was happening. The Polish troops thought I was a German soldier, and the Poles, who been treated by the Germans almost as badly as they treated the Jews, hated the Germans. Who knew what they would do to me?

My buddies, the non-German-speaking American soldiers, were allowed to leave.

I sat in a chair for over an hour in the middle of the tent, all alone and under armed guard—sweating it out. I imagined all sorts if horrors they could do to me. Knowing how much the Polish hated the Germans, they might even put me in front of a firing squad.

Finally, American M.P.s arrived in a Jeep, and fortunately they had a Polish-speaking German to explain that I was not a German soldier but a German-speaking American soldier. Luckily, they believed him and set me free.

By this time, after having walked what seemed like a few hundred miles plus being in that nerve-wracking situation, I was exhausted both physically and emotionally. I was hungry, too, because we hadn't eaten since early that morning. Luck was with me again for the M.Ps didn't make me walk back to Fürstenfeldbruck, but let me hop in the back of their Jeep for the ride back.

Post-war life in Fürstenfeldbruck, and probably all German cities, was rough. I saw people, men mostly, scrounging for cigarettes, picking up long butts from ashtrays, street gutters and even urinals. When American soldiers dumped leftover food into garbage cans, German men, women and children stood in line to pick out what was edible. Children everywhere demanded *Kaugummi* (chewing gum) as well as condoms, which they blew up like balloons. And now it was the German people themselves, not the Jews, who were not allowed to use the railways for travel. Consequently, German soldiers discharged from POW camps sneaked rides on top of the American troop-train cars to get home. Many German civilians were homeless—their homes having been bombed in the air raids. Women lost husbands and sons in battle. Men lost wives, daughters and parents in the bombing. The German people were a conquered people. We never heard a single "Heil, Hitler" uttered by these broken, vanquished souls.

Now that the war was over, there was no need for my skills as a radar operator/mechanics and "the brass" didn't know what to do with a soldier with my skill sets. So, instead of attaching me to an airbase, I was ordered to report to a signal corps. When I reported to the RTO (Railway Transportation Office) in Würzburg as ordered, I got the message that I was to go to Illesheim with the signal corp., and the officer in charge of the RTO requisitioned a Jeep and driver. When we got to Illesheim, there were no Americans in sight, so there was nothing else we could do but return to the RTO office in Würzburg.

We waited. Still there were no orders, so after much discussion, and because I could speak German, I was assigned the task of enforcing the rule to remove hitchhikers from the trains. They issued me a 45-caliber pistol and instructed me to use it only in an emergency.

My first attempt to remove POWs from the train resulted in defiant refusal. They flat refused to move, so I slipped the gun from the holster, held it shoulder high and ordered them to dismount. Again, no one moved. Indicating I meant business, I shot the .45 into the air. Nothing. Then, the bullet I shot in the air fell back to earth and hit one of the POWs in the leg. Scared now, they tumbled off the train top and ran in 10 different directions. I was concerned about firing the gun in a non-emergency situation and immediately reported the incident. I was told not to worry. In fact, I was patted on the back and told I did the right thing.

I was there long enough to become friends with the captain in charge, and when we had off time we often sat around over a beer and chewed the fat. I told him I was from a small town just 50 miles away, and I asked for permission to take a short leave of absence to go to Sterbfritz. I wanted to see it again. I wanted to see where I had lived and see if the war had changed it and the people who lived there. The captain agreed and made all the arrangements for me to use a Jeep from the motor pool.

On my way to Sterbfritz, I kept thinking about the past and something Bertel told me when we were together in Paris. She said that when she had recovered somewhat, she also felt the need to go back to Sterbfritz and Altengronau to see what had happened there. She wanted to see what it looked like now, after the war. She said it was so different, yet the same. The buildings were all there—all the same, but the people were different as well as the types of businesses that occupied the familiar buildings. Different people inhabited the houses. Where Jewish families once lived, German gentiles now resided. There were barely any Jewish faces to be seen.

Bertel said that Kirst was still operating the grocery business in our house. She knew that our parents held a mortgage on the house payable to a bank in Schluechtern and that the bank rented the house to Kirst. The rent covered the mortgage payments from the time we were forced to leave. She was able to find that principal balance was 20,000 marks. She also told me that she had given an ultimatum to Kirst to vacate the store and apartment, which he had not, and Bertel was not strong enough to enforce her ultimatum.

The first thing I did when I got to Sterbfritz was to find Kirst. He recognized me at once and showing feigned excitement and happiness to see me, he tried to hug me. I pushed him away and at the same time pulled my .45 out of its holster. I ordered him to step back. It must have scared him because he started to babble nervously about how often he thought about us, and how friendly he always was towards us. How much he really liked us.

Stopping him in midsentence, I reminded him of the reason I had to leave Sterbfritz in the first place. Did he remember the sign he made that forbade Jews to climb the stairs to our apartment? Did he recall that he had me, a 10-year-old boy, put in jail for having altered the sign? His face contorted, he begged me to forgive him, explaining that he was forced by the Bürgermeister to act the way he did.

I couldn't believe what I was hearing. I couldn't believe the lies. Did he think I was stupid enough to think his words were true? I responded by telling him that I would be in Sterbfritz for only a short time, but when I returned, he had better be out of the house. If he was not, I would personally throw him and his belongings into the street—or worse.

I went into our house and found that the Recker family, who were decent people, were still living on the second floor. The third floor was now occupied by what was called *Fluechtline*, refugees from the eastern part of Germany. I told them they could stay because they had nowhere else to go. I made a short courtesy call at the Reckers' and had a cup of ersatz coffee with them before leaving. As I passed by the first floor, I again stopped long enough to tell Kirst he better not be there when I came back.

Our house in Sterbfritz was still the most modern in the village. Most houses had running water in the kitchen, but only three houses had a bathroom. The house was still beautiful and not only in my eyes. It was a Sterbfritz showplace, and Bertel and I wanted it back along with the fields and the meadow.

We were the legal owners, but I wanted to pay off the mortgage so that it would be ours free and clear. I went to the bank and was told that if the principal of 20,000 marks was paid, the property would be returned to our parents or their legal heirs.

Raising 20,000 marks was easy. A carton of cigarettes brought $200 in scrip money (all Americans stationed in Europe were paid in scrip especially minted for our military). The exchange rate from these so-called dollars was 10 marks per dollar. I had no problem acquiring 100 cartons. Even if the soldiers didn't smoke, at the PX they could buy their weekly allowance of cigarettes anyway. I was one of those guys and several of my friends were happy to give me their allotted PX cartons as well. I had the cash in hand in no time.

The next step was to get copies of my mother and father's death certificates. Abraham Schuster's death was recorded in the archives and the reappointed Bürgermeister (mayor) of Sterbfritz was the same man, Mr. Loeffert, who had been the mayor before Mueller's tenure. He immediately gave me my father's death certificate and another for our mother, a document that stated simply that she died in the east.

From that time on, Heinz Dittmar Schuster and Bertel Schuster were the legal owners of our parent's property, and we were legally able to expel Kirst from our house. My next trip to Sterbfritz, two soldier friends accompanied me just in case Kirst was still there and gave me a fight, something I think he was planning to do. He hadn't moved out and when he saw three American soldiers with .45 caliber pistols in their holsters, he became instantly agreeable and vacated the store at once. That done, I left Sterbfritz for

Altengronau. Next on my list of things to do was to visit my father's grave.

The cemetery was just as I remembered, sitting atop a mountain with only a narrow dirt road accessing it. The incline was so steep that even my Jeep couldn't make it all the way to the top, so I got out and walked the 50 or so yards to my father's grave.

Miraculously, the cemetery had not been harmed by the bombing; however it was overgrown with weeds and new seedlings. The wooden gate was partially rotted away and the Chevera Kadisha house was in dire need of repair.

I had no problem finding my father's grave; I remembered exactly where it was. Standing over the headstone that bore his name, Abraham Schuster, I recited the Kaddish and placed a small stone marker on the headstone as is Jewish custom. The several minutes I stood there seemed like hours, and I felt a closeness to my father that I had not felt since I was a child. I wanted to tell him everything that had happened—how Uncle Moritz Steinfeld had saved my life. How the Germans had stolen our money and property. How brave my mother and sisters were, and that he would have been proud of us all. I wanted everything that was in my heart to spill out into his. I wanted him to know I loved him. That I would always remember him with love, respect and gratitude for everything he had done to make me a man.

I could hardly drag myself away, but it was time. I wiped the tears from my eyes with the back of my hand and began the short trek down the hill to my Jeep. I wasn't Abraham Schuster's little boy any longer. I was a man and a soldier, and I had a job to do. I was expected to report back to Wüerzburg before dark, and I did.

When I got back to the RTO, they said I was to be assigned to the nearest air base. The next day, I got my orders to report to Sergeant Major Sleyback at the Ansbach Air Base, and this time I was driven in a US Army staff car to a building that was a former Luftwaffe two-story brick barracks.

When I got there, the first question Sleyback asked me was, "Why are you here?"

"I really don't know, sir," I replied. "My M.O. was radar training for B-29s." With that, I handed him the official pouch I was carrying.

"By any chance, do you speak German?" he asked. I nodded that I did.

"Then we can use you," he said. "I'll assign you to my building, and you'll bunk with Sergeant Johnson. His room is next to mine."

Sergeant Sleyback told me his Jeep was outside and gave me directions to his building. The ground floor was high above street level, and to reach the ground floor I had to walk up a flight of concrete steps to the main entrance. My duffle bag was heavy so I decided, what the hell? I'd drive the Jeep up the steps. I put the Jeep in four-wheel drive, and up I went. At the same time, the company communications officer, Captain McDonald, walked by and yelled, "What the f— are you doing?"

Caught in a foolish act, I stuttered my reason—that my bag was too heavy. With a look of disgust, he said that if I had nothing better to do than to drive up stairs in a Jeep to report for duty in the communications office.

"Yes, sir," I replied meekly.

The communications office, where the telephone switchboards were located, was in a former German bunker. Before returning the Jeep, I drove to the bunker to see what was going on. The switchboards were being operated by two PFCs. Next to the switchboard was a room that was the hangout for the two telephone repair and installation guys. After a 15-minute lesson on how to operate the switchboard, I was made a telephone operator. Two or three days later, four English-speaking German women arrived to take over switchboard responsibilities, and I was now told I was to become an installer.

As the US forces marched through Germany, the Signal Corps. installed telephone lines any way they saw fit, slung over rooftops or trees if need be. Wires were everywhere. We found that the German communication system was an elaborate one, and we would need the help of German technicians to integrate their system with ours.

Captain McDonald had the solution: Send Corporal Schuster to Erlangen to work with the local Germans in incorporating our system with theirs—and to learn how to climb a 30-foot telephone pole. The second day of my new job, I found myself on top of a pole with the German technician. As if that weren't scary enough, from somewhere a shot was fired. I don't know if it was fired at me, the American, or the other guy, the German. I only know I was so scared I finished the job done as quickly as I could and shinnied down the pole.

One of the benefits of being a switchboard operator was that I had access to phone equipment and could make calls almost whenever and to whomever I wanted. I had the Franks' number in Paris, but I had to get the area code, an easy task since I knew people at the American Telephone Company closest to the French border. Once I had the area code, I dialed the number and got through to the Franks. Luckily, Bertel was there, and we were able to speak.

I filled her in on my trip to Sterbfritz, seeking Kirst, the Reckers, the refugees and my visit to Father's grave. It was great being able to tell her all that had happened and from then on we arranged to talk almost every evening.

Interestingly, it was at this time in my service career that I became an early version of the "M*A*S*H" character, Radar. I could find anything anybody wanted. The first time I was able to get hard-to-find items was for the female German telephone operators. Their biggest postwar complaint was that they couldn't find sanitary napkins, and they asked me if I could get them cotton for that purpose. It's odd that this kind of conversation didn't embarrass me, especially since I was very interested in one of the phone operators, a beautiful young girl named Erna Löesh. But I found the cotton they wanted and from then on I was the purveyor who supplied the girls with cotton from the base dispensary. Nothing embarrassed me.

Soon after I arrived at Ansbach, I saw a posted notice addressed to all Jewish personnel. A Jewish chaplain was to arrive from Nuremberg on a given date, it said. All Jewish personnel from the base should meet with him at the Officer's Club dining room. I, along with approximately 20 other Jewish officers and enlisted men, met with the chaplain who explained that because there weren't enough of us we couldn't have a permanent Jewish chaplain. However, he said he would come once a month to conduct Friday night services and be available for consultation on religious matters.

"Does anybody read Hebrew?" the chaplain asked the group. Mine was the only hand that went up.

"Corporal Schuster, will you be able to conduct Friday night services during the weeks I can't come?"

"Yes, but I can't sing," I replied, meaning that I couldn't be the cantor as well.

"Well, any attempt you make will good enough for me," he said with a laugh, placing this additional duty on my shoulders.

Now, we had to find a place to hold services. The next day, one of the German employees said there was an old synagogue on his street. I couldn't believe it. I remembered living through November 9, 1938, Kristallnacht, when all the synagogues were torched. So the next day I asked for and was given permission to leave the base to investigate. To my surprise, the synagogue was right where he said it was. The sanctuary was trashed, but I was happy to have found it even in that condition. It was a synagogue, a place of Jewish worship, and miraculously one of the Safer Torahs (Holy Scriptures) was still in the ark. I hardly could believe my eyes.

How was it, though, when all the other synagogues had been burned to the ground with Torahs slashed and thrown into the streets, that this synagogue was saved? I later learned that the reason was that the adjoining house had been the Ansbach S.A. commander's residence. Had the synagogue burned, his house would also have gone up in flames, so he made sure the synagogue was protected.

The ancient Torah was saved by the local cobbler who had a shoe repair shop across the street. The cobbler was a kindly, Christian man who had been employed by the synagogue as the janitor and the Shabbos goy before the 1935 edicts. On November 9, when all the other synagogues were in flames, the cobbler rushed into the synagogue and took the ancient Torah from the ark. Then he surrounded it with clay roof tiles and buried it in his vegetable garden behind his house. When Germany surrendered, he unearthed the tiles and replaced the Torah in the ark.

When I met him, he told me the story with gladness as well as sorrow. Gladness that the synagogue had not burned, and that he was able to save the ancient Torah, but sorrow that none of the former Ansbach Jews, his friends, survived to return to the synagogue. With our services, the synagogue would once again ring with the voices of Jewish people, but the voices of the Ansbach Jews had been silenced forever.

With permission from the base commander, I met regularly with the regional military governor who assigned civilians to clean up the synagogue and make it usable. Then, I sent word to the chaplain in Nuremberg who came at once to see it himself. He was as astonished as I had been that the building and the Torah had survived, and with gratitude, he sanctified the building to make it ready for services the following Friday. It felt wonderful to make the old building a place of worship as it had been in the past, to hear Hebrew prayers once again fill the sanctuary.

As irreligious as it now seems, at the time, the synagogue restoration and the unearthing of the Torah felt like a strike back at the Gestapo. Making Judaism live again in Germany seemed as if we had just sent an "up yours" message to Hitler and his henchmen. Somehow, the gesture felt holy. Very holy, indeed.

By ourselves, the 20 or so military Jews were too few to fill up the building. We needed more Jews to attend services, and I had a plan. I had heard about a displaced persons camp close to Ansbach that was in a former German army base and housed roughly 50 liberated Jews. It was run by an organization called UNRAH, a group that operated temporary living quarters for liberated survivors and was headed up by the man who was New York City's mayor, Fiorello Henry LaGuardia.

We went to the camp to meet with the people living there and to invite them to come to our services that Friday. Most of them were from Hungary, and most spoke no German or English. Hebrew, however, is the universal language of Jewish religious services, so everyone was able to participate. With the new synagogue in operation, we no longer had our services on the base, and it was decided to hold services only when the chaplain came and could conduct them.

During my station duty in Ansbach, approximately 50 miles from Nuremberg, the investigations and preparations for the Nuremberg Trials were in full swing. A notice came to the Ansbach command that requested a German-speaking American soldier to work as an interpreter for the C.I.D., which was in the process of arresting all former SS and regular army soldiers who were involved in atrocities, many of whom had not been released and were hiding within several Wehrmacht prisoner of war camps. I was ordered to

Erlangen to report to the C.I.D. officer in charge there. My job was to work with a designated C.I.D. officer to check each POW for double-lightning tattoos under their arms. While not all SS officers had the double-lightening tattoos, we found many who did, and we sent them to trial for their war crimes. Information was easy to get. With the power of a pack of cigarettes, there was always a snitch willing to cooperate and give us information.

The Nuremberg POWs were as tough and as ugly as the POWs at Camp Beauregard but with a difference. The Nuremberg POWs were largely homosexuals, and while I never saw them engage in actual intercourse, I witnessed hand holding, kissing and other intimacies. Perhaps they had been homosexuals all their lives or perhaps the loneliness of prison and being far from home and family made them resort to homosexuality. I don't know.

When I reported back to Ansbach, they no longer needed me as a telephone installer, but I was not yet given a new assignment. In the interim, I requested and received a 10-day furlough so I could go to Paris once again to see Bertel. I billeted near the Franks' house in a large hall that was a former hotel now being leased by the U.S. military. The hall had several beds as well as footlockers and hanging space for uniforms. It also had a dry cleaning and laundry service that was made available to U.S. military on leave.

As always, I came well equipped with my duffle bag full of valuable items that could be sold on the black market. Mr. Frank told Bertel where she could to go to sell the loot to get cash. There were almost always several buyers for anything. In fact some items were scarce, buyers tried to outbid each other.

Bertel had not tasted ice cream since well before the war, and she hungered for it. Luckily, part of the PX had been turned into an ice cream parlor, and more than anything Bertel wanted to go to the PX to savor a dish of ice cream.

I told the ice cream parlor's manager the story of our family and of finally finding my sister alive again. Touched, he broke all the rules and allowed my sister, a nonmilitary person, to join me in the PX ice cream parlor. Not only did we enjoy the best ice cream a la American style in sundaes, banana splits and ice cream sodas, Bertel was allowed to buy anything she wanted as long as we paid with dollar scrip. We wolfed down ice cream until we almost made ourselves sick. I remember it like it was yesterday, and I can still remember how good it tasted.

When we weren't gobbling down dishes of ice cream, we'd enjoy an evening at the famed Bal Tabarain cabaret in Paris, go to movies as well as attend an opera or two. Together, Bertel, Ilse and I often walked through the still-beautiful parks, the only ugliness was that these places were often frequented by French prostitutes, many having had to turn to prostitution when the job market went to ruin because of the war. Once, a French prostitute called out to me and told me she was much better than either of the two women I was with.

The war was over but in Russia, Joseph Stalin was the Russian leader and on February 9, 1946, he addressed the "voters" as well as other Supreme Soviet leaders at the Bolshoi Theater. In his speech, he stated that "it would be wrong to think the Second World War broke out accidentally or as a result of blunders committed by certain statesmen, although blunders were certainly committed. As a matter of fact, the war broke out as the inevitable result of the development of world economic and political forces on the basis of present-day monopolistic capitalism. Marksists have more than once stated that the capitalist system of world economy contains the elements of a general crisis and military conflicts, that, in view of that, the development of world capitalism in our times does not proceed smoothly and evenly, but through crisis and catastrophic wars."

On February 11, 1946, the American consulate reopened in Paris after having been closed from before the war. With the affidavits for support from Sam Schuster and me in hand, my sister and I were greeted by the consul general's American secretary who immediately showed us into his office. It was Bertel's birthday, February 11, and when the consul general learned that, as a birthday gift, he granted her a visa to enter the U.S. immediately.

"Not only do I wish you a happy birthday and give you the gift of a visa as a birthday present, I also wish a happy birthday to one of our great presidents, Abraham Lincoln, who was born on February 12, 1809." He said. "Even though his birthday is tomorrow and not today, I wish you both a very happy day."

Bertel was doubly pleased. To be granted the visa as well as finally realizing her dream to be reunited with her family in America made that day the most wonderful day we had had since before the war.

With a letter from the U.S. consulate, Bertel was able to get immediate permission to enter England, which she did. She had wanted to go to England not only to see if there was a war-bride ship available on which she could book passage, but to say thank you to some very important people.

On the top of her list was to look up the British soldier and his mother who had forwarded her letters to me in the states. They were easy to find, and her visit was filled with tears as well as thanks. She was so grateful for the kindness of the British soldiers and their families. More than forwarding letters, the soldiers had offered immediate medical aid to the freed camp prisoners as well as any clothing and food that could be found. Those who needed it most were the first to get sustenance.

In addition, the soldiers recruited their families in England help contact the prisoners' family members. As much as my sister hated the Germans who had mercilessly murdered so many fellow Jews, she equally loved the people who, for no personal reward, went out of their way to help survivors.

But getting to America would prove to be harder than anticipated. Checking on ship's passage to America, she found that the information she had been given in Paris was wrong. She would not be allowed to board the war-bride ship in England as she expected and was told to return to Paris and recheck with the consulate there. Returning to Paris, it was not long before she was successful in gaining passage to America, this time on a war-bride ship from France.

In general, I was feeling a lot better about the human race. During my visit with Bertel, she told me about a German couple, righteous gentiles, who at great personal risk helped provide food and other necessities to the home for the aging where she had worked before being taken to the camps. Had they been caught, they would have been shot in the street. Their families may have also been killed.

Though it was tricky, the plan they devised worked. Mother would leave an empty suitcase in the yard behind the house, and during the night the couple, with the help of others, put potatoes, bread and vegetables into the suitcase. There was not enough food to feed all the old people in the home, and without the help of these people, they would have gone hungry. In an already weakened condition due to their age, they may have died from hunger or malnutrition. Mother insisted on paying for the food and while they took the money, the risk they took was far greater than the small sum of money they received.

I have lived a long life, as of this writing 82 years, and I still regret not finding those people after the war and helping them however I could. I had money galore; I could have helped. I will go to my grave regretting that I did not.

My sister also told me that prior to being sent to the camps, for safekeeping, they gave all the valuables they had left to them by the Nazis to a Frankfurt family named Ehler. When the war was over,

Bertel looked them up, and they said they still had everything in a trunk, just as Mother had placed them there. Going through the items, I was not surprised by the choices Mother made in things to keep. Included in the treasure chest, as I called it, was one of my mother's favorite dresses. She probably hoped to wear it again someday when the war was over. There were the linens and tablecloths my mother so cherished—still done up in pink ribbons as if they had just been taken from her linen closet. Underneath the tablecloths were several crocheted items our *Oma* (grandmother) had lovingly made in addition to man's dress suit. Papa was already dead. Was she saving it for me to wear in better times? We'll never know. What struck me was that she fully expected to survive, and that she saved what she thought she would need again someday. During the summer of 1946, I shipped all the items to New York except the man's suit, which I kept with me. If Mother had saved the suit for me, she had been right to do so. I needed that suit.

With reluctance, I bade farewell to Bertel—she was on her way to the United States—I was on my way back to complete my military service at Ansbach Air Base.

At Ansbach I had lot of work ahead of me. Each barracks had a dayroom; it was more like a recreation area that was used strictly for relaxation. Sergeant Sleyback wasn't happy with the dilapidated furniture there, so he asked me if I could find a new couch, chairs and tables. I thought there wasn't anything wrong with them, and that they were good enough, but the boss was the boss. Instead of going to the expense of replacing what appeared to be sturdy and serviceable couches and chairs, I figured it would be cheaper and easier to re-cover the furniture than to replace it. The furniture just needed a little new fabric here and there. But when I asked about upholstery fabrics in Ansbach, I was told there were none to be found. However, the proprietor of the largest shop told me about a supply house in Hanau that would be our best bet in purchasing the needed materials.

With permission, the upholsterer and I drove to Hanau to find the shop and to buy whatever we could. Finding enough fabric to cover the furniture, we loaded our weapons-carrier vehicle with the new purchases and back to Ansbach we went. Within two weeks, the upholsterer had refinished the two couches and several chairs, and they looked better than new at less than half the price.

Now, we needed some tables and a bar. Through my contact with the upholsterer, I found a cabinet shop in the city where we got the things we needed. Not only did we get a bar, tables and a storage cabinet for our allotment of liquor, we had a magnificent dayroom with bright new chairs and couches. Everyone was impressed that I was able to accomplish my mission so fast and so efficiently. My secret was in knowing the right people to ask. It's not what you know, it's who you know. True then; true now.

More people than ever were coming to the dayroom bar because it was so much more pleasant. Prankster that I was, I thought I'd have a little fun. One evening, when it was packed with people, I put on the civilian suit I had stored in my footlocker, combed my hair to look like Hitler's, used a burned cork and blackened a small mustache. I did a great Hitler imitation, clicking my heels and giving the Hitler salute. I made Hitler look ridiculous and it was my way to get back at a man who had caused so much damage and death. I knew Hitler couldn't bear to be ridiculed, and I had people rolling in the aisles laughing at him.

But for someone in the room, it wasn't so funny. Whoever it was called the M.P.s, who immediately asked me, in broken German, to raise my hands above my head. I could tell they thought I was the real Hitler, and I couldn't help but giggle.

Speaking in English, I said, "It's only a joke," rubbing off some of the charcoal mustache and ruffling my hair. Everybody there was laughing by this time including the M.P.s who left laughing too. However, I had to fill out a form they handed me. From then on, no more Hitler jokes. No more forms.

In late 1945, wives were allowed to accompany U.S. officers. Adjoining our air base was Katterbach, a village built to house Goering's Luftwaffe officers' families, and which now housed American families.

Colonel Kirkendall had the largest and most exquisite accommodations, and when Mrs. Kirkendall came, she requested items she wasn't able to bring with her. Sleyback, knowing I could get almost anything, asked me to find the things she needed and wanted, the most important on her list being a radio.

The radio was no problem, but I went one step farther. Not only did I get a radio, I got a radio combination record player. Just like Radar, I was able to locate anything. As far as the colonel and his deputies were concerned, I was the greatest gift they had at the Ansbach 9th Air Force base. To keep the brass happy it's always smart to keep the wives happy.

When I returned from my most recent trip to Paris, I reported to Sergeant Major Sleyback for a new assignment. He and Master Sgt. Johnson came up with the idea of an Enlisted Men's Club for dancing, basketball and various other indoor activities. Permission from Col. Kirkendall set us on the path of finding a suitable venue, and with the help of the Ansbach mayor we found a large indoor arena that had been used for livestock auctions. The arena had an earthen floor with bleacher seating all around, and everyone thought it would be too difficult to convert into a club. But I saw it differently. I knew it could be done.

The hard part was finding carpenters, plumbers, electricians and all sorts of people to do the construction work. I contacted the cabinetmaker to engage him as my foreman. Not only was he the proprietor of the woodworking company, he was also a master builder.

My concept was to build a large wooden floor that would cover the existing earthen floor. On two sides, we would build two decks that were capable of supporting tables and benches as well as seating areas. The cabinetmaker said it was possible to accomplish, but difficult. He hired 30 carpenters from the surrounding area as well as plumbers and electricians to get the project underway.

We needed lumber and not far from Ansbach was a lumber mill from which we immediately requisitioned all of their lumber for our project. But heavy rains during the spring of 1946 left the lumber soaking wet; it had to be thoroughly dried before it could be used. To do that, I requested a number of portable heaters from the quartermaster and with some arm-twisting by our command, we got what we needed. During the time it took to dry the lumber, I had all the existing bleachers disassembled and saved all the material that could be salvaged. With two 6x6 trucks from the motor pool, we made repeated trips to and from the lumber mill and got all the wood assembled and ready for construction to begin.

We purchased a heating system in Holland as well as the additional electric components that we needed. Without the cabinet maker's knowledge and experience, I could never have accomplished this immense job. With the venue construction well under way, my attention next turned to acquiring things like beer mugs. What would a social hall be without frosty beer mugs? These we imported from Belgium, and Sleyback was able to requisition a C-47 to pick up the mugs from Brussels. Everything arrived just in the nick of time for the huge grand opening.

We had our club ready for opening night on July 16, 1946—a record three-and-a-half months from start to finish. It was wonderful! At each end of the arena, beer bars served 3.2 percent beer. I engaged talent for a floor show that we found through a company in Munich.

The show was actually a circus without animals—something like the Cirque du Soleil today. It was a huge success.

The structure had an extra bonus for Williams and me. We had the carpenters build a bedroom underneath the platform, a bedroom that not only had a big double bed but the convenience of a bathroom and toilet, one that had been salvaged from the former livestock arena. There was no shower, but who cared? It was comfortable and private, and a place I could use to rendezvous with my girlfriend, Erna Löesh, though as time went on I very seldom slept in there. I more or less lived with Erna in her apartment.

Erna, if you remember, was one of the telephone operators I got to know when I was a telephone installer. She was a lovely German gentile woman whom I was immediately attracted to. She was not only beautiful, but kind and generous, and I knew she had grown to love me. After a time, she talked about marriage, something I knew from the start I would never enter into with her. Erna was a gentile and I was Jewish. Because of my upbringing and because so many of my family died just for being Jewish, how could I turn my back on my faith and my heritage now? It would be as if Hitler had won. I couldn't do it. I was determined that when I married, it would be to a Jewish woman, and that our children would be raised Jewishly. Being Jewish, living a Jewish life and raising Jewish children was primary for me. Coward that I was, I didn't tell her that and led her on.

I am ashamed of the way I treated her, and if I could go back in time I would handle it all differently. I would have told her that I couldn't, no wouldn't, marry her, and after that if she still wanted to continue our relationship, it would have been her decision. But I never gave her the information she needed to make that decision. Up until the day I set sail for home, she thought I would come back for her. I didn't, and I never wrote to her or spoke to her again. Erna, I'm sorry.

CHAPTER
SEVENTEEN

I felt like I was an important person and highly respected by both our troops and the German people. Articles were written about me in the military newspaper, Stars and Stripes, and German publications. The Enlisted Men's Club was so successful that on weekends U.S. military and their spouses came from as far away as Munich to enjoy our shows. As a Stars and Stripes article noted, "Ansbach, which used to offer slim entertainment, is now becoming a good deal brighter thanks to Sgt. Schuster." The complete text of the two articles written about the new Enlisted Men's Club follow:

CLUB TO OPEN

In 4 to 5 weeks, a spacious club for enlisted men of the Ansbach Air Depot will open in Ansbach. Manager of the club Sgt. Henry D. Schuster, or better known as "Kraut" by his friends, has been devoting his entire time to shaping what was once an indoor stadium for displaying stock into an EM hotspot with seating capacity of 600 to 800 people. The whole project could be done much more rapidly if tools and materials were available. "Kraut" Schuster is well qualified to organize civilian help since he speaks German fluently and having lived a good part of his life in this country he understands how to handle the people in his charge.

The bleachers which seated spectators at the "county fair" are being ripped out to make room for several different levels of floor space. The main floor will be either of tile or hardwood depending on which Sgt. Schuster is able to acquire. Beer and cokes will be on sale at the 2 bars which are at each end of the hall. On week nights there will be a German band at the club and on Saturday nights the place should really get "groovey" when a G.I. band takes shifts with the civilian musicians.

The EM Club will be open from 18:00 to 22:30. A check booth will be available for checking in hats and coats. Beer and coke will be brought by civilian waitresses to the tables. Men are allowed to escort their female acquaintances. Among the attractions which are planned for the club are dances, boxing matches and basketball games. The club will be a success only if the men who use it cooperate in keeping the place orderly. Sgt. Schuster with the assistance of CPL. Williams and M/Sgt. Raymond C. Buck are working hard to make the club something that will be appreciated by the men of the Ansbach Air Depot. The sergeant major, M/Sgt. C.H. Slayback, has provided appreciated assistance in getting the new club started. The EM Club in town can be a "good deal."

EM OF THE WEEK

The grand housewarming of the new EM Club located a half block from the 1ˢᵗ Division Tech School in Ansbach is the result of the supervision and hard work of S/Sgt. Henry D. Schuster of the 42ⁿᵈ Headquarters Squadron. His ability to surmount the problems of obtaining materials and labor proved to the EM Club Council what they already knew—that Sgt. Schuster had the necessary "know how" for the job.

It took "Schus" 10 days to procure skilled workers and materials, but an additional 3 weeks were used for drying out lumber that had become saturated during the rainy spell. Supervising the actual construction job of converting a former show place for pigs and cattle into a spacious club was something new to him, but natural aptitude and his qualifications for handling German help made the task possible. "Schus" was born in Frankfurt, Germany. He saw the rise of Hitler Tyranny and his parents lost their lives in a concentration camp. Henry managed to escape from Germany in 1939 when he was 15 years old, and fled to France where he saw the first Nazis arrive in Paris. Schuster sailed for America in 1941. His knowledge of Germany and the German people make him a logical candidate for the job.

Next on his list is the construction of a 1ˢᵗ 3 graders' club, which will be built in the former Drexel Gardens.

Ansbach which used to offer slim entertainment is now becoming a good deal brighter thanks to Sgt. Schuster.

The war was over and everyone was in a party mood. A lot of the get togethers were in an apartment building originally built as German officers' quarters. It was not far from the club, and it had been requisitioned by the United States military for German civilians who worked for the American forces. The second floor was used for living quarters for our base telephone operators.

Five German women lived there, and they had lots of wild parties. I was able to buy a gramophone and records that we used for dancing. On one occasion, the drinking really got out of hand. The apartment in which we had the party had a balcony and Master Sergeant Scruggs (who was really loaded that night) was dancing with a girl named Maria on the balcony. Somehow, he lost his balance and fell against the railing, which gave way. He tumbled head over heels into the flowerbed two stories down. We rushed down the stairs to see how he was and found him alive and breathing, maybe thanks to the alcohol, but his leg was badly broken. Because he was so drunk, we didn't dare take him to the base hospital, so we carried him to his Jeep and drove him to one of the local doctors. The doctor put a plaster cast on his leg, and only then did we take him to the base infirmary. By this time, he had sobered up a bit.

Seeing what a mess Scruggs was, I took this as a wakeup call for myself. I figured it was only a matter of time before I would find myself falling into a flowerbed from a second-story balcony like Scruggs because by now I really enjoyed drinking. It had become a way of life for all of us. Realizing how dependant I was on booze was when I stopped drinking altogether.

While our parties were pretty tame, in retrospect, sometimes other parties turned ugly. An American officer was accused of raping a civilian woman. At his court martial, non-English speaking witnesses were required to testify, and I was told to be at the trial as a translator. The officer was found guilty and immediately was shipped back to the states. I never found out his punishment.

Of the five women in our party group, only Agnes had a German husband. Maria, Stella and Anni now had American boyfriends. They were widows whose husbands had been killed fighting against the Allied forces for the "Vaterland." I wonder how their dead husbands would have felt if they had known their wives were now partying with the enemy. My girlfriend, Erna, was the only one who had never married.

In 1945, American soldiers were not allowed to marry German girls, but I remember there were several weddings between U.S. soldiers and non-German women anyway—Polish and Hungarian women who were living in Germany. I was a witness at a buddy's wedding for which I had to lie about my age. Witnesses had to be 21 years of age or older, and I was only 19. Now that I think of it, that probably makes their marriage illegal.

By September 1946, I had enough points to be discharged. Colonel Kirkendall summoned me into his office and tried to talk me into re-enlisting and to stay in Ansbach. He tried to entice me with the promise of a promotion to officer. He also told me he would recommend me for a medal for outstanding service as well. In addition, the Bavarian military governor also asked me to stay as a German civilian employee.

My life was way too comfortable and my relationship with Erna was getting much too serious. In addition to wanting to marry within my faith, I was too young to get married. What's more, I felt a strong sense of responsibility to help care for my sister who was now living with cousins in New York. After days of soul searching, I decided to go back to the states and leave the Army and Erna forever.

I labored over my decision and how to cut off my relationship with Erna. My first thought was to tell her before I was shipped out, but I didn't have the courage nor the heart to go through with it. So, I said nothing. Aboard ship back to the states, I felt so bad about it I talked to a Catholic chaplain. His reply was, "Do what your conscience tells you." That wasn't much help, so I finally came to the conclusion to do nothing and hoped that it would be best that I just faded from Erna's life. I hoped that it would take her less time to get over it than it did me.

We sailed from Hamburg on a troop ship with 1,300 men who were divided into individual packets. Because there were not enough officers to take charge, the captain decided to appoint several sergeants with the rank of staff sergeant and up as take-charge guys. I was one of the guys appointed and was now in charge of 100 soldiers.

What goes around comes around, as they say, and on the ship was the very same Shepherd Field drill sergeant, the anti-Semite who had treated us so badly and who hurled abusive language at me and the other Jewish soldiers. He was a buck sergeant, and because I now had some rank, he acted as if we were old buddies, slapping me on the back and offering me cigarettes. I knew that sooner or later he'd hit me up for a favor, and he did. He asked if he could be my deputy. I couldn't believe this guy. He had the audacity to ask me for a favor after the lousy way he treated me back in the states. But, I kept my cool. I declined his request and calmly reminded him of the abusive way he had treated me and the other Jews. Then I told him that though he could not be my deputy, I did, in fact, have a job for him. He could be in charge of KP. He murmured something under his breath and left. What goes around comes around.

On the way across the Atlantic, the guys in our cabin started a poker game that continued, nonstop, for the entire trip over. When anyone dropped out there was always someone else to take his place. This marathon poker game may be eligible for a Guinness Book of World Records mention.

Our ship docked at Newport News, Virginai, and we were greeted by an Army band. What a sight! Many civilian families were there to meet loved ones, but we were immediately taken by buses to Camp Polk in North Carolina, so I'm not sure how much time they got to spend together. After several days, the separation process began. First, physicals to check for VD. Those infected had to report to the base hospital for treatment prior to discharge. The process was orderly and quick. Those who wanted to re-enlist were first, getting $300 in discharge money. Off they went for a two-week furlough. The rest of us were interviewed in alphabetical order.

I was directed to a booth for my interview. The entire process stopped when the sergeant who interviewed me told me I would not be eligible for discharge until I settled a 35-cent debt.

"What the hell are you talking about?" I yelled. He told me that he didn't know and first had to check into it. The next day he told me it was money I owed for a broken cup. Then I remembered the cup-throwing incident. I should have carried the tray of cups to the dishwasher. Instead, I figured it was quicker, and much more fun, to throw them. I guess I did owe the money, so I happily paid my 35 cents, got my $300 and railroad ticket for Shreveport as well as my honorable discharge papers and army lapel pin. It took about three days to get through the whole discharge process. Before leaving Camp Polk, I joined the inactive reserve and was ordered to report to a reserve unit in Shreveport.

CHAPTER
EIGHTEEN

I cashed in the railroad ticket and took a Greyhound bus to Jacksonville, Florida. Tante Matilde was my host for the short visit in Jacksonville. So much had changed. Both Ilse and Martha were now new mothers and their children, David Landes and Melvin Gottlieb, were about 6 months old.

From Jacksonville, I took a bus to Shreveport with a short stopover in Monroe, Louisiana to visit with my Army buddy named Cook. Cooky and I were inducted on the same day and were together all through basic training, Truax Field, Chanute Field, Boca Raton and Williams Field in Arizona. But instead of Europe, his overseas duty was Japan. Cook had no intention of going to college, and he was now a plumber's apprentice, following in his father's footsteps. With the high cost of plumbing these days, it was probably a wise decision.

During my two weeks in Shreveport, I stayed in the vacant apartment over Uncle Dave and Aunt Leah's garage. There were so many people to see, so many lives to catch up on. First, I went to see Sam and Perle. I wanted to thank them for allowing me to stay with them for my first three years in the United States, a debt I could never repay.

Sam was happy to see me. My relationship with Perle was still cold, but I was an adult now, and she managed to treat me with respect. Sam tried to convince me to make my home in Shreveport, offering to give me one of his liquor stores that he still owned. Near retirement, Sam had sold Schuster's Produce to a competitor but happily kept himself busy with all his other endeavors. It was a kind offer, but I declined. I explained that my intention was to go to New York and set up housekeeping for my sister and me. I think Perle was relieved.

Two days later, Colonel Lyons and Betty arrived with their two sons from Washington D.C. They, too, had offers to make and wanted to give me the chance to go to school in Virginia. I could stay with them to keep expenses down. Again, I had to decline the very generous offer.

Julius and Sue still lived in the house behind the riding academy. During my stay in Shreveport, I visited with several of my former schoolmates, and when I went to Byrd High School I was treated like a returning hero. The principal asked me to speak at a special assembly and to wear my military uniform. The war just over, kids were hungry to hear what really happened, especially in the concentration camps. When they found out my background, I had their complete attention. I wasn't just some guy who had read about the war. My family and I had lived the drama. You could hear a pin drop.

Before leaving Shreveport, I retrieved a box of mementoes and personal belongings that were in the closet of my old room at Sam and Perle's, and Sam was kind enough to buy me a brand new suit with two pair of pants and several shirts. Sam was a kind man and enjoyed what his money could buy for himself, but he also was generous, often buying things for other people for no other reason than that he wanted to.

When I said goodbye to Sam Schuster that day, I didn't know it would be the last time I would ever see him alive. In 1952, Sam was killed in an auto accident. Wheelchair bound, he was a passenger in a truck being driven by someone else. When the accident occurred, Sam was thrown from the truck and killed instantly. I hope he knew how grateful I was for all the good things he did for me. I hope he knew I loved him.

I never did report to an Army Reserve Corps. I left Shreveport on a Continental bus for McGee, Arkansas, changing buses in Monroe and traveling the same gravel road that I had traveled to McGee years before to visit family. Tante Emilia and the rest of the family were glad to see me. Max and Arnold were still in the same business, selling their various articles to the little country stores in southern Arkansas. Norbert was in the cattle business with his cousin Hamburger. Jean Sue was now living in Memphis with her husband.

They all had plans for my future and wanted me to stay with them and go to Southern Arkansas State College. Again, I explained that my intention was to go to New York and make a home for Bertel and me, but I stayed in McGee for about a week and then went to Bloomington to see my Uncle Moritz and Aunt Toni Schuster.

I owed most of my gratitude to Uncle Moritz Steinfeld because without his insistence on taking me out of Sterbfritz, I cannot say what would have happened to me. The schoolmaster's cruel "pranks" could easily have caused my death, and if not, a boy as young as me was of no use to the Nazis who would have killed me without a second thought because I was a "useless Jew."

CHAPTER
NINETEEN

It is now long after the war years, and I am far away in both time and space from the horrors of Nazi Europe. I didn't set up housekeeping with my sister Bertel in New York as I had planned. Still the older sister, Bertel took charge of her own life and accepted an offer from Milan and Mina to live with them.

Seeking employment, her first job was as a baby sitter with an American journalist and his wife. A miserable man, it was not long before he told Bertel that the German Jews deserved what happened to them. In a rage, she quit the job and walked out.

At her next attempt at employment, she snagged a job as a sewing machine operator with an upholsterer, a job that trained her in the craft of upholstery and required a minimum knowledge of English. It was there that she met Harold Kale, a handsome man who worked in his brother's upholstery factory. Over time, Bertel and Harold found they had much in common and looked at life from the same perspective. While she was learning English, Harold bought books for Bertel to read that not only gave them wonderful topics to discuss while helping to improve Bertel's command of the English language. Shared time and shared thoughts created a shared attraction and love. Theirs was love whose bonds grew stronger over time. Harold and Bertel were married in May 1947, a marriage that has, at this writing, lasted 61 years.

I got acceptance into the Manhattan Technical Institute for electronics and got a part-time job at S. Klein in the Square as the fur department cashier. I remember the salary was 57 cents an hour. I was lucky enough to find a room with a German couple for $20 a week that included breakfast and dinner.

I didn't marry the lovely Elfriede Meyer. After I was discharged from the army, I recontacted her but now she had a boyfriend—a great guy she eventually married. We have remained good friends, however, and over 60 years have managed to talk on the phone and see each other as often as we can.

Nor did I go back on my resolve and marry the sweet Erna Lösch—a fine woman whose only imperfection was not being Jewish. When I married, I chose a lovely young woman by the name of Anita Kleiman, a friend of a girl named Tillie, one of my co-workers at S. Klein. Anita also worked part time at S. Klein.

Anita was young, only a 16-year-old junior in high school. When I first met her and she caught my fancy, I didn't know just how young she was; she appeared much more mature for her age. I was 21 and guessed she was nearer my own age but I didn't find out how young she really was until she allowed me to meet her family. They took a dim view of her dating a man so much older than she and let me know it.

Anita was beautiful. She radiated health and vitality with a peaches-and-cream complexion, shining brown hair and a figure that would stop traffic. When I bumped into her at the employee locker room at S. Klein, I wasted no time asking her out.

Our first date was a movie at the Paradise Theater in the Bronx. I remember it well. There were more stars in my eyes than on the theater's ceiling, and there were plenty of stars on that ceiling. It couldn't have been more romantic. I have no idea what the movie was; we talked through the whole thing. I held her hand, not wanting to move it for fear she would pull her hand away. My arm was cocked in a strange angle that cut off my circulation. It started to feel prickly with sleep. Then I couldn't feel it at all. I was so happy to be holding her hand that only the building on fire would have made me move it. When the lights went up, it was 20 minutes before I felt life flood back into my sleeping appendage.

I didn't want to leave her yet, so I asked her if she wanted to go to Krum's ice cream parlor. Krum's was known for serving the biggest, gooiest ice cream sundaes in all of New York, and I must have ordered the biggest and the gooiest. We ate ice cream until it was coming out our ears. But we also talked, talked, talked, and I realized that this beautiful creature was as lovely inside as she was out. This time, my heart was really lost.

Recovered from my sugar overdose, I walked her home and up the five flights of stairs to her family's apartment. She lived with her parents and grandfather, a gruff man who immediately let me know she was underage. My ears were getting frost bite from the chilly reception I got, so I made my apologies and headed for the door, with Anita trailing close behind.

"Can I kiss you?" I asked at her doorway.

"No," she replied without hesitation. The girl knew her mind, and I was impressed. I also knew in spite of her age, I would see her again.

It was a difficult courtship, geographically speaking. I lived in Manhattan and she in the Bronx. To see her I had to take the subway, spending an hour after school and work, and I often fell asleep on the trip. I traveled the route so often, I almost became a fixture. The cleaning crew saw me so regularly and they knew, if I fell asleep, when to wake me for my stop.

The Manhattan/Bronx commute lasted for a year or two, but by now, Anita's parents took pity on me and often offered to let me stay the night. A roll-away bed was brought out from the closet where I often slept until morning, rising early and hopping the train back to my part of New York.

Economically, things were looking up as well. One day, when the teacher didn't show up for my class, the dean asked me to teach in his stead. He knew I had excellent grades and could wing it if I got in over my head. But I knew the material well and had no problem. I was able to explain the lesson simply and answer questions clearly. I did so well that the next day, when the teacher failed to show a second time, the dean asked me to continue teaching the class for the rest of the semester, a job that paid $125 a week—big money in those days especially for a part-time job.

I was still seeing Anita and her family warmed to the idea that we would probably get married. Their only requirement was that we wait until she was 18, a stipulation with which we both agreed. It was 1947. I had taken Anita to her junior prom and that year I escorted her to her senior prom.

On prom night, I remember how beautiful she looked in a floor-length pink hoop-skirted gown, and how my hands shook when I tried to pin the gardenia corsage to a dress with off-shoulder cap sleeves. I was head over heals in love with Anita. While I had had many infatuations and one love affair, this was different. This was the woman I wanted to share my life with and have children with. She was young and beautiful; she was intelligent and wise beyond her years; she was kind and compassionate—and she was Jewish. Best of all, she loved me back.

Our engagement party was on New Years Eve, 1947/1948, and 25 close friends and family members wished us well and helped us celebrate our love and our upcoming marriage. Anita turned 18 on August 31, and on Sunday, September 12, 1948 at 2 p.m. we were married at Temple Zion in the Bronx. Now, pleased with the marriage, and with me, and happy that we had waited until Anita was 18, *both* Anita's parents walked her down the aisle and gave her away in marriage.

She was a vision. Her dress was a shimmering silver color, and she wore long white gloves that her father had made. On her tiny feet were maroon, round-toed high heel shoes with a baby-doll strap, and she wore a stylish Juliet cap with a grey veil. She was the prettiest girl I had ever seen and in a few minuets she would be my wife. Few things in my life have moved me as much as seeing her walk toward me with all the love I felt for her reflected in her own eyes. Our vows exchanged, the glass crushed under my heel and the reception over, we left for our honeymoon at a resort in the Pocono Mountains. Nine months and two weeks later, our son Alan was born.

We were to be the parents of four children: Alan born on July 1, 1949; Kenneth on September 30, 1951, Michael born on December 21, 1952 and Reneé, our only daughter, born on June 22, 1955. Our family was complete.

Supporting my burgeoning family, I took a variety of jobs: everything from opening a retail store that sold salvaged items like hot water heaters and other plumbing fixtures as well as new items like surplus paint—all at bargain prices. In 1969, I closed the store to become a homebuilder, and in my career constructed over 100 quality-built homes. When the bottom fell out of the housing market, I took a job as a construction manager for another company with offices in Denver, San Francisco and Honolulu. It was my job to travel to all the offices except for the Saudi Arabia office—where Jews were not allowed. Over the years, I did well financially, and when it came time to retire, Anita and I chose Las Vegas as our final home. In November 1993, we bought a lovely house in Las Vegas in a beautiful master-planned community just a few miles west of the famed Las Vegas Strip.

CHAPTER
TWENTY

My story didn't end there. Once established in Las Vegas I found there were 35 other Holocaust survivors already living in the Las Vegas Valley with many more coming each year. Nevada's lack of a personal income tax combined with the mild winter weather beckon many retirees, and Holocaust survivors are no exception.

Retired Holocaust survivors have many of the same issues and problems that other retirees have like finding affordable housing, solving unique health care issues, and obtaining convenient and inexpensive transportation to and from doctor's appointments and shopping venues. In addition to the day-to-day concerns that need to be addressed, Holocaust survivors are faced with special issues. Many suffer from survivor guilt, many have mental health problems related to the horrors they witnessed and experienced, and many still suffer from being uprooted from a society familiar to them to one that was new, strange and sometimes unwelcoming. Some fear the same anti-Semitism that enveloped Germany could overtake America. Almost all fear the demise of the state of Israel, without whose existence the entire world would be a dangerous place for Jews in spite of the good life America has provided for us. Most

Jews feel in their hearts that Jewish genocide could happen in any country, and that Israel is the last refuge against anti-Semitism.

Knowing first hand the Holocaust survivor's state of mind, Anita and I organized a small group of survivors we knew to form the Holocaust Survivors Group of Southern Nevada, a group that meets frequently to socialize, talk, listen and offer each other advice. Always accompanied by platters of good Jewish and American cooking, many times we would meet in each other's homes. We laugh, we cry, we hold on to each other for support.

As word got out, other survivors joined our ranks. Each month, new survivors move to Las Vegas and more and more join our group. It is estimated that over 300 Holocaust survivors reside in the Las Vegas Valley today. We have outgrown the ability to meet in our living rooms and now look for larger spaces to accommodate all the survivors who wish to join other survivors.

Some of the support we give each other comes in the form of just being there for those who need it; other times it comes in the form of helping to get monetary restitution from the German government and money to hire German lawyers who will take their cases. I have spoken on radio and television and have given newspaper and magazine interviews in order to find other survivors who don't know about our group as well as to raise money to pursue restitution claims. I also have spoken before many groups and organizations about what being a Holocaust survivor means. So many people of all age groups don't know about the Holocaust, which is an ignorance that is truly astounding.

Anita and I have spent many hours at the Las Vegas Jewish Family Service Agency helping survivors fill out masses of paperwork required by the German government to begin the restitution process. Once the process is underway, often additional paperwork is required, and I spend even more hours helping survivors who are feebled by torture, sickness as well as age, try to get what restitution they can, restitution that is rightfully theirs. It's a long process, but one that is well worth the effort when checks are received, property returned and justice served. It's a labor of love, and one that I am emotionally and morally required to undertake not only as a fellow survivor but as a fellow human being. My dear wife, Anita, has taken my burdens as her own and has worked as hard as I have for the benefit of other Holocaust survivors.

Then, in 1997, while on a trip to Israel, Anita and I visited Yad Vashem where we saw my mother's name and my sister's name on the memorial plaque. It was this plaque that was the inspiration for a personal quest that would take me seven long years to bring to fruition. But come to fruition it did, and on March 21, 2004 I led a delegation of 22 American Jews in placing three plaques that would honor the 32 out of 100 Sterbfritz Jews who were murdered by the Nazis for no other reason than that they were Jews.

The three plaques were placed on the grounds of the Lutheran Church in Sterbfritz opposite a WWI memorial that honored five Jewish soldiers; on a monument outside a cemetery wall in Altengronau, Germany; and on a monument inside the cemetery itself.

It was an overwhelmingly emotional day for me to not only pay tribute to my slain family but to all the other Jews from Sterbfritz who died in the Holocaust, and whom I knew well when I was a child. It was a time of being reunited with people who shared the same horrifying experiences at the hands of the Nazis. It was also a time of forgiveness for those who turned their backs on us, and a time of understanding for two of my sons, daughters-in-law and three grandsons who were present at the dedication. The plaques and the monuments are, indeed, a moving reminder for generations to come that this time in history must never be forgotten.

They say everything happens for a reason, but I'm not sure I agree. I see no reason why six million Jews were put to death. But lessons were learned all the same, and for me it was lessons in forgiveness, tolerance of differences in skin color, faith and ways of life. It also taught me the importance of contribution. We live in a world of many sorrows, not just Jewish sorrows, and everyone must contribute to diminish if not eliminate the sorrows of others. Those who have are obligated to contribute to those who have not. Those who possess the God-given capability to function effectively in this world are obligated to contribute to those who cannot. It is a responsibility, not a choice. This is a philosophy that the Holocaust and becoming an American taught me, and one I wish to pass on to my children, grandchildren and anyone else who will listen. If there was ever a reason for the Holocaust, it is that.

CPSIA information can be obtained at www.ICGtesting.com
Printed in the USA
BVOW081225111112

305176BV00002B/35/P